Four Visions
of
America

Four Visions
of
America

Erica Jong
Thomas Sanchez
Kay Boyle
Henry Miller

Capra Press
Santa Barbara

FOUR VISIONS OF AMERICA copyright © 1977 by Capra Press.

"Report from Lock-up" copyright © 1977 by Kay Boyle,
"The Real Cowboys and Indians," copyright © 1977 by Thomas Sanchez,
"East-West Blues" copyright © 1977 by Erica Jong,
"A Nation of Lunatics" copyright © 1977 by Henry Miller.

Cover photographs:
Thomas Sanchez by David Harden
Erica Jong by Peter Trump
Kay Boyle by Dan Tooker

LIBRARY OF CONGRESS CATALOGING IN PUBLICATION DATA

Main entry under title:

Four visions of America.

    CONTENTS: Jong, E.   East-West Blues.—Miller, H.   A nation
of lunatics.—Boyle, K.   Report from lock-up. [etc.]
    1.   Authors, American—20th century—biography—addresses,
Essays, lectures. 2.   United States—civilization—20th century—
Addresses, essays, lectures. I.   Jong, Erica   East-West Blues   1977
PS 129.F 64   813'.5'408   77-1382
ISBN 0-88496-126-5
ISBN 0-88496-127-3 pbk.

Published by CAPRA PRESS,
631 State Street, Santa Barbara, California 93101

CONTENTS

"*Where there is much desire to learn, there of necessity will be much arguing, much writing, many opinions; for opinion in good men is but knowledge in the making.*"

—JOHN MILTON, *Areopagitica*

Kay Boyle, center, among Cesar Chavez's Farm Worker marchers on Modesto. Joan Baez Sr., is on her right.

KAY BOYLE

REPORT FROM LOCK-UP

I

It may be that none of us can ever get out of the solitary confinement we've condemned ourselves to (out of fear, out of pride, out of loneliness) until we find ourselves in actual prisons of iron and stone. We constructed these prisons, just as we did our own individual places of detention, building them on the ruins of other epochs, accepting as viable the *oubliettes* of other centuries, other continents. When everything else we have put our hands to is gone, the granite and iron cemented by our pitiless morality will remain as monument and gravestone to our time. The walls of Troy and Limerick were built to keep the invader out, but we have built walls to keep the lost and bewildered among us out of our line of vision, walls to seal our fellow-citizens away. The interior decorations include the ancient wrist, ankle, and waist chains, and we have added the modern touch of bullet-proof glass. What are we going to say to history about our fear of facing one another in a courtroom or in a taxicab except through this impregnable barrier which half of our countrymen make use of to outwit the other half? We can listen to Dylan singing his ballad of the cutting down of

George Jackson, singing (and tears stand in my eyes every time I hear it) that "the whole world is one big prison yard" where "some of us are prisoners, the rest of us are guards," and not believe it until the moment that we too see the landscape through windows fitted with iron, and hear the doors locked behind us, and before us, and around us. That is the moment when you come out of your own solitary confinement once and for all, and if you're lucky there's no way for you ever to go back again.

William Carlos Williams, poet, doctor, essayist, is one of the gigantic figures we have to honor of a man escaping while still young from his own solitary cell. It was not through the experience of prison that he escaped, but through his coming to an understanding of the conditions of his patients' lives. "I lost myself in the very properties of their minds," he wrote, "for the moment at least I actually became *them*, whoever they should be, so that when I detached myself from them at the end of a half-hour of intense concentration over some illness which was affecting them, it was as though I were reawakening from a sleep. For the moment I myself did not exist, nothing of myself affected me. As a consequence I came back to myself, as from any other sleep, rested." *

II

There were two women in the room called lock-up which they put me in that evening in 1968, two white women sitting on their cots, talking to each other across the intervening space, who did not look in my direction as the deputy led me in. I was handsomely fitted out (as were they) in a grey prison dress that hung unevenly nearly to my ankles, and on my bare feet were tennis shoes, once white, and two sizes too large. Over my left arm I carried two worn sheets, a pillow case, a greyish towel, and in my right hand I held a toothbrush and a small cake of soap. Once the deputy in her smart uniform had gone and locked the door behind her, I turned the mattress on the third cot to find which side was the least stained, and then I made my bed. I laid the folded khaki blanket under the flat pillow, and I lay down on

---

* *The Autobiography of William Carlos Williams*, New Directions, N.Y., 1967, page 356.

the flat, flat cot whose springs cried out in pain. From then on I became the two women who were supplying each other with the facts and figures of their dreams as they sat on their cots in the narrow room.

There were not young women, and not beautiful women. One was a fleshy, weary-eyed Canadian who talked of the Yukon, and when she gestured the dimples came and went in her plump elbows, the fat tied as if by strings to the invisible bone. Her mouth was a small trap-door between her sagging cheeks, a door that snapped open and closed on the words she spoke. The place they'd head for when they got out would be Whitehorse, she said, but they would go even farther, the two of them pushing always deeper into the wilderness until they finally reached the mines.

"Silver, lead, zinc, even gold, you know," she was saying.

"I really like your accent. I really do," the other woman said.

"Silver, tungsten, and coal, you know what I mean?" the Canadian woman went on with it.

"What's tungsten?" asked the woman from maybe Brooklyn, maybe New York, who had wandered this far without a compass to keep a rendezvous in lock-up with a woman she had never laid eyes on before. "What's tungsten?" she repeated, and she began to laugh, the round little face between the dry, yellow slabs of the page-boy bob framed by an inch of grey. "Sounds kinda indecent to me."

"It's part sheelite, tungsten is," said the Canadian. The trap-door of her small, trapped mouth hung open, black as the hole of Calcutta, and her flesh jerked with laughter.

"Oh, did I hear you right? Did you say you-know-what?" shrieked the other woman. "Did you say 'shee—' or am I hearing crazy?"

"Listen," said the Canadian, snapping the trap-door abruptly closed, "we can't waste any time now. We got to keep pushing ahead. There's the Yukon Territory, and beyond that there's the Klondike, where the gold is waiting. That's where the men are. That's where they've got to be," she said, and now her voice had taken on another dimension. Now she was speaking of the real, not the dream. I was no longer someone lying on a cot across the narrow room from them, face turned to the wall, lying there in a long grey dress with the hem ripped half-way out, and dirty tennis shoes on, nameless and without history, listening to what they said. I had become nothing more than a bunch of rags there hadn't been room to stuff onto the dog-sled as they urged the huskies on through the driving snow, bent on getting to where the men were before night fell. "They've been mining silver and panning gold," the Canadian woman said, "and they're crazy for women, just crazy for them," and the other woman could be heard rubbing her palms together in glee.

And then the mood abruptly changed, as if the hypodermic of dreams had been suddenly snatched away, and the teeth of the lady from Brooklyn or New York began to chatter like castanets in her head.

"Do you think I'd get on up there in the cold and all?" she asked, plaintive as a child. "I'm American. Always have been. I love every state in the union, only some are better than others for professionals," she said.

"We can get our hair touched up at the roots before we go," said the Canadian in answer to the question that was asked.

"They'd have a choice—me light, real honey blond, or was once anyway, and you the brunette type," the other woman said, trying to make it weightless as feathers so that the sound of desperation would go away. "I might have trouble with the language in a place like that."

"There won't be any trouble!" the Canadian woman shouted. She must have jumped up from the cot then, and standing erect on the runners of the sled she began cracking the long serpentine of the whip over the flanks and the muzzles of the harnessed dogs as they raced over the hard-packed snow. "We'd pick it all up and get out quick!"

"I'd rather do business with the gold-miners than the ones come out of the coal mines," the other woman said. "I bet they're black all over, right down to their you-know-whats," and she gave a shriek of laughter, but there was the sound of something else in it now, sharp and jagged as broken glass.

"Gold's cleaner than coal, you're right about that," the Canadian woman said, her voice gone sweet with craftiness. "You can carry it easier, too," she said.

It was growing dark, but neither of the two women on their fierce ride toward freedom could stop long enough to switch on the single bulb that would tremble, faint with light, its twisted vein out of reach in the peeling ceiling overhead. Outside the barred window in the door, the hallway was as still as the grave, and if the sound of footsteps had come tripping down it, or the kindly face of a deputy brightened the grating, I would have sensed it there like a searchlight turned on us, and sat bolt upright on my bed.

"Please, lady, dear lady, why am I in lock-up? How do I happen to be here?" I would have asked her.

But beyond the door there was silence, total silence. Only in this one room did the panting dogs run wilder and wilder through howling winds, the steam of their breathing hot as fire on the forty-below-zero air. Whitehorse must have been left a hundred miles behind by this time, but the Yukon and Klondike and Indian Rivers were still to be crossed. One after another, the Canadian woman was naming them all, not forgetting Bonanza Creek, on whose banks there was more gold than gravel. She had the statistics, she said. Twenty-two million dollars in one year was what had been panned there, she was saying as the sled sped on, but she didn't mention which year or century. That was because she was too busy flailing the dogs in their desperate race against the falling night. Maybe in the middle of this room stood an outsized hour-glass whose sifting sand measured time, and she kept one cautious eye on it as she talked, but I wasn't going to turn my head to see. She was speaking of the Porcupine, and the Chandalar, not to mention the Tanana, all navigable, she said, as if navigating them was what she and the other woman were going to do. All tributaries of the Yukon, she added knowingly.

"The way I do it, I get them to buy a six-pack," the woman from New York or Brooklyn was saying in the accumulating dark, "and then we go up to the room, and while we're lying on the bed we get rid of a can or two, and then I let him—"

"I never lie down with them until I've got the knock-out potion into their drinks. Get it, 'knock-out potion'?" the Canadian woman chortled.

"I get a charge out of your vocabulary. I really do," the other woman said. But the Canadian woman's mind had turned to something else. She was trying to find a way now to cross the rivers lying ahead when there wasn't any moonlight available to put a shine on the ice, and no way to see the foot path over the torrents of water that had been turned to marble by the cold.

"Then I go through the pockets of their pants they've got hanging over the back of a chair," she said, "and if the pants and the shoes are in good condition, I take them along." She was speaking briskly enough, but the edge of the precipice could be heard in her voice. It was lying just ahead. "I'll kill anybody if they're blocking my way to that window over there. I'll kill anyone standing between me and you and the Yukon," she said.

"I never took anything but their wallets. That's all I ever did, bar none," the American woman said piously, and she began to cry in a stifled, piercing, child-like way. "I got to have a shot of something, I tell you. I got to have it."

"I'd kill anyone I thought was hiding it under the pillow over there, maybe hiding it under her blanket," said the Canadian woman, and suddenly she struck the wall with her fist, as if it was a face she couldn't bear. "Ask for it, ask for it!" she shouted so loud that it must have been heard a mile away. "If they have any hearts under all that regalia, they'll give it to you! Yell loud enough and they have to give it! I read that, it's a medical fact!" In the vast reaches of the nordic night through which she battled her way, she was ready to strangle the huskies one by one if they didn't run until their hearts burst in the cages of their ribs, carrying her to where she wanted to go. Despite the bars, she was going to get through the window that looked out on the darkening courtyard, stamping the life out of the bundle of rags lying on the third cot as she went, blazing her escape through prison-yard and over prison wall with its fine barbed wire worn like a crown on its granite brow. Before *rigor mortis* set in, she would throw the carcasses of the dogs, like sacks of bones, at anyone who tried to stop her, lifting them up by the taut curves of their bushy tails and flinging them at her pursuers in place of hand-grenades, in place of tear-gas cannisters, and the loud report of guns. "The facts and figures are on our side, and so are the statistics!" she shouted out of the fury of her advance across the black glass of the Klondike River. "They're thousands up there who'd stand by us, nearly twenty thousand!" she halloo-ed back to the woman from Brooklyn, or wherever it was, who had fallen and who now lay rigid, as if frozen, on the bare boards of the floor.

"Maybe up in the Yukon," the fallen woman whispered in what could have been her dying breath, "there might be men wanting to settle down. There might be some of them looking for women to make them good wives. Out of the lot of them up there, there might be some."

It was her own tears that stopped the sound of her voice, but the Canadian woman had no time or use for pity as she beat her savage tattoo on the impervious door. (Oh, lock-up, what a battle-ground of terror you are, and no stretcher-bearers to come and bear the mortally wounded away!) First she would slap the door with the flat of one hand, and then with the mighty fist of the other the steady, ominous rhythm would be hammered out.

"Two hundred and five thousand, three hundred and forty-six square miles, that's the size of the Yukon!" she roared. "Water surface two hundred and seven thousand and seventy-six square miles! Mt. Logan is nineteen thousand eight hundred and fifty feet high!" she shouted, the thousands, the hundreds, the odd numbers, beaten out in fury on the door. "What have you got on this side of the border to compete with that?" she cried.

"I love every state in the union," the other woman whispered from the ice floe of the floor, and her teeth were chattering again.

"Let me tell you this," said the Canadian woman, and she struck the door an even fiercer blow. "Five months of the year, five months out of every year," she said, and suddenly the remembrance of it must have changed the air she breathed, for her hands fell quiet, and her voice turned almost gentle in the trap-door of her mouth. "Five months out of every year the days are twenty hours long. I know every inch of it from the Arctic Ocean to Skagway and back again. Five months out of the year you can sit on a park bench and read, just like sitting under a neon light, you can read a newspaper at two o'clock in the morning," she said.

"Why do you want to do that?" the other woman asked through her chattering teeth. "Why reading a newspaper in the park at that time of night?"

"Because nothing in this country can compete with that, that's why!" the Canadian woman shouted, and now it seemed that the door of lock-up would have to split apart under her blows. "Where in the United States can you sit on a park bench and read a newspaper in the middle of the night, every night for five months? You can't sit in Golden Gate Park in San Francisco and read a newspaper all night, or in Dolores Park, but in Yukon Territory you can, I'll tell you that!"

"Well, keep it down, keep your information to yourselves, ladies," the deputy said from the safety of the hall, and she switched on the searchlight that would show them up for what they were: prisoners, just hallucinating prisoners, held fast by lock and bolt and key. "Get into your beds. Don't let me hear another sound out of any of you," the deputy said, not in anger, but in hopelessness at speaking words, whether she knew it or not, that make a language wither and die.

III

The next three days and nights were as dull as ditchwater, because in the lock-up room I was transferred to, the two prisoners who shared it with me had straight stories to tell. Very early in the morning I had been escorted up the hall to more spacious quarters, with the added attraction of being adjacent to the dark stronghold of The Hole. This room had three barred windows that looked out on the prison-yard, while the other had had only one, and for an instant at the crack of day I thought this might be a promotion. As in the first, there were three cots in the room, and two women, one black, the other white, sat on those they could call their own. There were no chairs in lock-up, but the authorized night-tables were smugly present, and into the drawer of mine went the prison-issue toothbrush that was fashioned to dissolve, lock, stock, and barrel, if you tried ramming it down your own or someone else's throat; and into my tidy drawer went my cake of pink soap, and the washrag and towel gone grey and weary in confinement. My sheets and pillowcase of the night before were purified still by the mercury-bright waters of the Klondike, and, worn as they were, bleached by the stainless drifts of Yukon Territory snow.

"Dear Deputy," I had asked the lady in her smart khaki as we journeyed up the hall together, "why have I been put in lock-up in the first place? In all my stays here, I was never considered dangerous before." But she had not answered. "Could I telephone my heroic attorney, Robert Treuhaft?" I had suggested in the instant before she click-a-locked us all in again, and she spoke her mind on that with an unswerving look at something else at the other end of the hall.

The girls sitting on the cot in the far corner was pregnant, and as I settled in in my domain she gave me a wan smile. She said it was seven months now, and that her husband was in prison on the men's side of our condominium. She had blue-veined temples and wrists, this girl, and long, light hair, and eyes the color of African violet petals, with the rings under them a lighter shade. When she said she was having trouble with the food that arrived on the metal truck that came creaking up the hall three times a day, you knew this was why there was little or no buoyancy left in her pastel-tinted flesh. Except for the grey prison dress and the split tennis shoes, she was a Marie Laurencin portrait painted like a mural there, perishable and frail, with the great windows of her eyes like delicately stained glass. Across the room from her, the large black prisoner, who had lain down now, dark and mountainous, on her narrow cot, sized me up in a minute and a half.

"I bet you could write me a good letter. I needs someone to write me a good letter," she said.

Possession is a mutable word, a word with a number of differently colored masks it puts on and then takes off at will. It can be blood red with rape, or brassy with wealth when domiciled in a safe-deposit box, or mad as a whirling fakir if you see it as witchcraft, and another time amorous as Venus in the embrace of love. Possession, black as a pit, black as The Hole outside our door, was what the Marie Laurencin girl and her husband were accused of, but she said, sitting there on her cot, that they'd never possessed anything at all. They'd never had very much money, and they'd been taking care of her sister's kids, she was telling me just before the cold globs of oatmeal and the sloshing cups of dark warm water that was breakfast came trundling up the hall. Her sister was off on a week's nursing job in Eureka, a graduate trained nurse, divorced, she said, and a guy they didn't know dropped by the house one evening. He was the one who possessed, but the Marie Laurencin girl and her husband didn't know it until after it all took place.

"I guess he was a pusher," the girl said, a little uncertain about the word. "He used the phone out in the hall a couple of times, maybe making contacts. We didn't hear what he was saying because my husband, he's a carpenter, he was sawing wood to make the baby a cradle. That was three weeks ago." She said it was on account of the baby that she worried about the food she couldn't eat, and I said there had to be a doctor here, even here there had to be a doctor. "There is a doctor," she said softly, "but I think he likes men better than women. I heard there were two women sick here at different times, and they could have got well, but he didn't get help to them in time."

"I knows one thing. I knows you could write that letter for me that I got to get written," the black lady called out to me, sweet as honey, from across the room.

I wanted to tell the Marie Laurencin girl a lot of things. I wanted to tell her about Angel Island and Alcatraz, but it didn't seem the time to talk about it now. I wanted to tell her about Bird Man's isolation

cell on Alcatraz that he'd been in for seventeen years, as if this would
make as light as thistledown the burden of weeks that she and her
husband would have to bear. There were straight little marks, each
fine as a thread and maybe half an inch high, marching the length of
his cell's walls, I wanted to tell her, and a few tiny horses, with their
forelegs lifted, and a few birds with their wings spread, scratched
there by his thumbnail. It was a Native American who had shown
me that cell on Christmas day at the time of the Indian Occupation,
and when I said that must have been the record Bird Man kept of the
months and the years he'd spent there, the young Indian ran his
forefinger across the marks. "Not months, not years! They were
centuries he was talking about. He was marking the centuries," was
what he said. In the times when prisoners were in every cell on the
island, instead of Indians spreading out newspapers and sleeping
there with their children now, the young man said that they must
have been like an audience in a movie theatre, sitting looking out of
the dark through the bars at the bright movie screen across the bay.
"Sometimes I see it like that," he said, "the prisoners watching the
real life of America being played. And then sometimes I think of it as
the other way round, and it was the men in the cells who were acting
out the history of America, and the people over there in San
Francisco was the audience, not applauding or boo-ing or doing
anything about it, but year after year just seeing it taking place."

And beyond Alcatraz, a little farther out in the bay, there was
Angel Island, and I wanted to tell the girls about the Chinese who
had been imprisoned there, and whose ghosts wandered the beaches
now, and knelt in suicide under the trees. *But what help or solace
would that have been to her? Once upon a time, I wanted to say to
her as I rocked her and the unborn baby to sleep, lots and lots of
Chinese men used to come to California, come looking for work

---

* In his novel, *Good Luck, Happiness and Long Life*, Shawn Wong writes: "Everyone (on Angel
Island) knows how to hang himself. There are no nails or hooks high enough to hang a piece of
cloth from and leap from a stool to a quick death. There is only one way: tie your piece of cloth
to one of those big nails about four-and a half feet off the floor, lean against the wall to brace
yourself, and bend your knees and hold them up off the floor. Then your bones will be
collected and placed on the open seas."

because the grasshopper and caterpillar and hummingbird tongues they were used to eating for breakfast had run out where they lived in China. Aside from that, they liked the idea of working outside in the clean, sunny air of California, laying railway ties. But they didn't know immigration prisons were waiting for them on Angel Island; they didn't know because the way Frank Chin's Tam Lim explains it: "Chinese are made, not born . . . (made) out of junk-imports, lies, railroad scrap iron, dirty jokes, broken bottles, cigar smoke, Cosquilla Indian blood, wino spit, and lots of milk of magnesia." *

And rocking, rocking, I wanted to say to the Marie Laurencin girl that there was really nothing serious to worry about here, nothing tragic, as there had been on Angel Island. "Do you know," I might start babbling to her, "that when the women and children finally managed to beg, borrow, or steal the money to join their men, they too were closed up year after year until the end of time, and the mothers stopped letting their kids go to the washroom to wash, because that was where the Chinese, made out of junk-imports and broken bottles as they were, had chosen to hang themselves? Well, that couldn't happen here."

Perhaps I ought to keep quiet about that, I thought, and also about Shawn Wong's great-grandfather saying to him in his dreams: "I left for San Francisco one month before my brother. In those days, ships were bringing us in illegally. They would drop a lifeboat outside the Golden Gate (Bay) with the Chinese in it. Then the ship would steam in and at night the lifeboat would come in quietly and unload. If they were about to be caught, my people would be thrown overboard. But, you see, they couldn't swim because they were chained together in the hold of the ship. My brother died on that night and now his bones are chained to the bottom of the ocean. No burial ever." ** That was prison, too, prison of a worse kind, not like the place we were confined to, but still it was prison, wasn't it? I wouldn't put this question to the blue-veined baby still to be born,

---

* From Frank Chin's play, *The Chickencoop Chinaman*, produced at The American Place, Lincoln Center, N.Y., in 1973.

** Page 262, *Aiiii-eeeee*, Anchor-Press/Doubleday, 1975.

but I'd just rock its mother back and forth, back and forth, making up lullabies for it and not saying a word about the great-grandfather who had whispered down the years to Shawn: "Do not send my bones back to China. Bury me here beneath my tears." *

Deeply embedded in the words of lullabies there is a shuddering sense of tragedy, it came to me then. I thought of Colin, *petit frère*, being promised a drink of water if he would stop crying and go to sleep while his mother was upstairs making cakes, and his father was having the time of his life sawing wood in isolation, far below. And there was the lullaby from somewhere in the South saying that way down yonder in the meadow a poor little lambie was lying with the bees and the butterflies picking out its eyes. "Hush-a-bye, baby, don't you cry," it seemed to me was how it went, but how could it have gone like that when the little lambie was bleating out "Mama, Mama," and Mama off nibbling clover somewhere? I remembered the bough breaking in still another instance, and down coming cradle, baby, and all, and it seemed to me for a brief moment that some of the poems the Chinese had written for their children and their children's children on the walls of their Angel Island prison rooms might be the cradle songs of solace I was looking for. It may even have been that the Chinese mothers sang those poems to the children they bathed in the tin basins of water carried so carefully from the row of sinks in the washroom to the dormitories so the children wouldn't have to see the dead kneeling temporarily there.

(But can you remember those poems carved in the wood by carpenter's nail or point of knife, or painted on by finger or brush dipped in melted tar? How do I know what I can remember, I answered myself. I only know that their knives, like their detention would be solved if these immigrants plunged knives into their own or one another's hearts. I can remember lines from their poems better than lines from Pound's Cantos, or from "Prufrock" or "The Wasteland." I can't recall the names of those who wrote them, and my versions will be garbled versions, such as:

---

* Page 260, Ibid.

He travelled far across the ocean on a long voyage,
Feeding on the wind, sleeping on the dew, and tasting hardship.
Even though Su Wu was detained among the barbarians,
There is hope that one day he will come home.
When Han Yü encountered a snow-storm he sighed
And thought of the years he was banished.
From ancient times heroes often underwent ordeals.

This poem is an expression of the distress
That fills my belly. I leave this as a memento
To encourage fellow-souls.

Or else:

It has been several full moons since I left my native village.
At home, the family stands at the door, eagerly looking for letters.
Whom can I depend on to pass the word to them
That I am well? Green waters surround the grassy hills
Of this island. If I ascend to a high place
And look far out, I still cannot see the shore.

The lines I was remembering might well fail to sound like poetry
in the little, porcelain ears of the Marie Laurencin girl, and despite
the cruel tradition of cradle songs, they perhaps did not even qualify
as that. What baby, born or unborn, would want to hear a Chinese
prisoner crying out: "My stomach is full of grievances, but whom can
I tell them to?" Or another one murmuring scarcely aloud: "Staying
on this island, my sorrow increases with the nights and days"? And
even less would the new-born and still innocent wish to hear, no
matter how beautifully the words were sung:

I can do nothing but frown
And feel angry at heaven.
When I am idle, I have a wild dream:
That the consent was given me by the contemptible westerner
To land on the continent of America.

But there was a lighter moment one prisoner wrote of, something
about the waves beginning to laugh "ha-ha-ha" as they broke on the
beaches.

From this moment I bid farewell to this building (he wrote),
And my fellow villagers are rejoicing with me.
Even if it had been built of jade, oh, my countrymen,
This building would have turned into a cage!

No, none of this would do.)

What would be encouraging to tell the Marie Laurencin girl about was all I had done in the times I was here before. I had been free as the breeze, working in the Rehabilitation Center garden, digging up iris plants and cutting their tough, green sabres off, and then splitting the earth-clotted bulbs in two. Like preschool children, we had been allowed blunt-nosed scissors to do our work, and trowels with rusted, crumbling edges. They trusted us, as God had once trusted Adam and Eve, and when we had replanted the multiplied iris bulbs at a gracious distance from one another, we had responded to that trust by returning the scissors and trowels to the appointed authorities. It was here I had learned that once every two years this must be done to iris plants so they don't end up strangling one another in the crowded ghettoes of their beds. And another time when I was here, I had even been allowed to hear through a crack between the boards of the garden fence Martin Luther King speaking outside the prisonyard. He had come all the way to the hinterlands to tell us we were doing the right thing. On other occasions I had been allowed to do kitchen duty, and at five o'clock every morning I would spring from my pallet and speed like a deer to the kitchen area, proud of always being the first to clap the mandatory canvas boudoir cap on my head. I had been authorized to boil dozens of eggs, turn a hundred pieces of toast over on the grill, and stir the oatmeal while it was still pulsing in the cauldron, and no questions asked. But this time I had been hustled into lock-up, and I didn't know why I was here.

"Maybe they thought someone might try to spring you," suggested the black woman from where she lay on her cot across the room. "I heard two prisoners was sprung right out of this room last week."

"They sawed through the bars over there in the bathroom," the

Marie Laurencin girl said quietly. "That's why there's plywood nailed across."

If I had spoken of Alexander Berkman then, perhaps the walls of lock-up would have opened wide and let in a presence that would have changed the look of what we were; but I couldn't bring myself to begin. If I had said he'd been sixteen years in prison, more than half of them in solitary, and he had come out not only sane, but as well a compassionate, humorous man, would that have been of any help to the two women locked up with me here? I could tell them that Berkman's longing for liberty had so obsessed him night and day that it finally became "an exclusive passion, shaping every thought, molding every action"; *but would that have any bearing on the fact that the black prisoner wanted me to write a letter for her, and that the Marie Laurencin girl wouldn't be able to eat the oatmeal when they brought it up the hall? "The underground tunnel masters my mind with the boldness of its concept, its tremendous possibilities," Berkman wrote, but even if we embraced that conception, where were the tools with which to start our tunneling? "The world of the living is dim and unreal," Berkman went on writing. "Escape is the sole salvation," **and even though I believe every word Berkman has ever set down on paper or spoken aloud, I still didn't know whether escape from prison meant for him escape from the unreal world into the real, or from the stone and iron reality of prison into the world of fantasy which even Berkman made the error of calling liberty.

But the moment had come now when I must cross the room to the cot on which the black woman was reclining, and tell her I didn't have any paper, or pencil, or pen. When I stood beside her, she heaved her great weight up on one padded, black satin elbow, and the broken springs of the cot moaned in pain.

"My public defender, he got me my commissary privilege," she said. She reached out to pull open the drawer of her night-table, and she brought out the ruled pad and the ball-point pen. "I got to keep in touch with him," she said.

---

*_Prison Memoirs of an Anarchist_, page 330, Schocken Books, N.Y., 1975.
** Ibid., page 356.

It wasn't a very long letter that she dictated to me, but it was important to her that the spelling and the punctuation be exactly right. "Legally right," was what she said. She had a singular confidence in me as she lay there, monumental and onyx-fleshed in her grey dress that many had worn before her, for I could have written anything at all. When I had it all down, I read it aloud to her, to the sound of the breakfast truck creaking up the hall.

> "Dear Sir," it went. "The gentleman who was stabbed to his death in the Flamingo Bar on Monday night, which I plead not guilty to by reason of self-defense, had thirty dollars of mine in his pants pocket, the left one. I don't see no reasons why his widow should get that money that was mine. The gentleman and I had been going steady for six months, and the widow had no accessory to it."

I thought maybe she didn't mean the word "accessory," but she said she did. When the letter was done, she folded the sheet of ruled paper over and put it in an envelope, and she gave me a long dark look.

"What you in for?" she asked, and because of the nebulous dimensions of my crime, I lowered my eyes before her gaze.

"For demonstrating," I said. "I'm serving thirty-one days on weekends and holidays. That's so I won't lose my job."

"Demonstrating about what?" the black woman asked.

"Well, a lot of us sat on the steps of the Induction Center in Oakland," I said, explaining it almost in apology. "We just sat there, hoping the draftees wouldn't climb over us and go in. We were demonstrating against the war in Vietnam."

"Against the war in Vietnam!" she said, her voice gone high in incredulity. "Ain't you never heard of national honor?" she asked.

IV

I don't remember what I said or didn't say in the next three days and nights to the Marie Laurencin girl who couldn't eat and to the black woman whose cot springs sighed under her weight when she got up and when she lay down and when she turned over, before she was transferred out. There were things I wanted to tell them both about, but it isn't easy to say to people who have other things eating at their hearts that there is a history of women speaking out before judges and juries, so there is no reason to feel any loneliness when you stand up there to say your own small piece. There was a woman my aunt drew a picture of, and the drawing my aunt made became a postage stamp in time, and letters mailed in that particular year had the picture on them of a little woman with a small, black bonnet on her head and a red shawl drawn around her shoulders, walking entirely alone up the steps of the Capitol building in Washington D.C., and although you can't see it in the picture my aunt drew, she is holding a scroll in her hand. Never were steps more cold and bare than those this woman mounted, and never were columns more forbidding than those standing massively on either side of the dark door. The scroll she carried bore the signatures of 20,000 Americans who were asking that women be allowed to vote (and in the end that petition wasn't considered valid because the 20,000 names were those of women and not of men). Maybe a few people here and there that year noticed the picture of Susan B. Anthony on the postage stamp, printed long after she was dead; and perhaps not only women noticed, but other painters, other artists, who in that instant felt like a blow the total courage of a woman so small to the eye that you had to take a magnifying glass to be able to make out her bones.

But instead of mentioning that, it might have been better if I'd just gone on telling the Marie Laurencin girl and the black woman about the times before when I'd worked in the prison annex with the others, all of us busy putting patches in the seats of the male prisoners' overalls, or buttons on their grey prison-issue shirts. It was there that the chorus of young, young voices kept on warbling: "I bin in an outta this place so many years, I don try countin em no more," or: "This time I took the rap for my kid sister, but none of us, we don go roun makin no announcements bout why we're here. At firs, a long time back, I use go roun askin who done what, but after a while you don bother askin no more cause everybody done just bout the same"; or saying: "It ain bad, not here it ain. You gotta bed with sheets, an you can quit hustlin whiles you in, and you gits three meals a day. I knows which deputies goin be like my momma to me and which ain. Here is jus somewheres you come back to res up fore you goes back outside and git busted again. Tha's been my life since way back, an I got no complaints"; or maybe saying: "There's two things I knows a lot about, an one's women an th'other's dope. When youse in here, you gets to likin women, an thas cool. You in here for you reasons like I'se in here for mine. We both believes in them, an soon as I gits out, I go back, do my thing, and you gits out an go back doin yours . . ."

Somewhere, far away, Bob Dylan was perhaps still singing: "They were frightened of his pow'r, they were scared of his luv. So Lawd, Lawd, they cut George Jackson down," but I wasn't able to hear him, and no one else seemed to be listening, perhaps because it was never one of his smash hits. In the same way, down through the decades, scarcely anyone seems to have heard Susan B. Anthony saying in the courtroom: " . . . I shall earnestly and persistently continue to urge all women to the political recognition of the old Revolutionary maxim: 'Resistence to tyranny is obedience to God.'" And while I was thinking, or merely believing, these things, there was a cautious tapping on the barred windowpane set in the door, and I saw a girl's black face there, her dark eyes seeking us out. I got quickly up from my cot and went to where she was.

There was more than one face at the barred window now. There were two, then three, then four or five, girls coming back from breakfast, passing lock-up on their way to work in the annex, where I was no longer allowed to go. The eyes were fierce, or gentle, or else troubled with sorrow, and at times they darted quickly, warily away to see who might be coming up or down the hall.

"What th hell they put you in lock-up for?" came the hushed voices through the crack of the door, through the keyhole; or else the words took shape in silence behind the glass: "Wh-a-a-a-"—with the mouth wide open—"th-h-h"—with the rosy tongue curled behind the bright white upper teeth—"he-l-l-l"—in a scream no one could hear—"the-e-e-y"—with the mouth stretched in a grin, only it wasn't grinning—"d-o-o-o t-o-o-o y-o-o-o-o?"—with the lips pursed for kissing.

The eyes that kept skittering this way and that were the same that had seen to thread needles for me in the glorious freedom of the sewing-room, but they were sharp now with a different, darker precision. In the instant before these prisoners took flight, they pressed their mouths against their side of the barred glass, and on my side I put my lips against theirs, and the misty shapes of our embrace stayed a long time there, a long time after the two deputies had cleared the area of all human sight and sound.

I don't know what I actually said and what I only intended to say to the Marie Laurencin girl and the black woman before they took her away. It may have been that I mentioned Paul Goodman writing of Alexander Berkman that he was one of the beautiful human spirits which the regimes of the world cannot put up with. * It may have been this tribute by a man who had never known him that brought Berkman back into the room with us and started me talking about the birds he had lived with and loved. In one of his letters (one written on January 15th, 1900, and got out *sub rosa* from solitary), Berkman says: "I write in an agony of despair.... You remember my feathered friend, Dick. Last summer the Warden ordered him put out, but when the cold weather set in, Dick returned. Would you believe it? He came back to my old cell, and recognized me when I passed by. I kept him, and he grew as tame as before—he had become a bit wild in his life outside. On Christmas day, as Dick was playing near my cell, Bob Runyon—the stool, you know—came by and deliberately kicked the bird. When I saw Dick turn over on his side, his little eyes rolling in the throes of death, I rushed at Runyon and knocked him down." ** So Berkman was put in solitary again. And then in June of that year, a time when "Unfledged birdies

---

* *Prison Memoirs of an Anarchist*, by Alexander Berkman, Introduction, page xiii, Schocken Books, N.Y., 1970.

** Ibid., page 363.

frequently fall from their nests," Berkman was able to procure two starlings. "Old Mitchell is in ecstasy over the intelligence and adaptability of my new feathered friends," Berkman wrote, "but the birds languish and waste in the close air of the block; they need sunshine and gravel, and the dusty street to bathe in . . . . One day the Warden strolls by and joins in admiration of the wonderful birds . . . . 'Who trained them?' he inquires," * and on that day Berkman pleads for and is granted permission to take the birds out for ten minutes every morning, provided he stays near the greenhouse, where there is sand for them to flutter and shower in. If he crosses the deadline of the sidewalk or exceeds his allotted time by a single minute, he will go back into The Hole again.

What is it about birds, I asked myself, that made such disparate prisoners as Berkman and Bird Man turn to them in their confinement, one in the Western Penitentiary of Pennsylvania, the other on Alcatraz? Bird Man, twice a murderer, Berkman, a man who had failed in his attempt at assassination, both found solace (if that is anything like the word) in the small, swiftly beating hearts and the clinging threads of the feet of these fragile living things. (Fragile, my eye, I thought, for weren't they powerful enough to spread their pinions and outwit any wall, and cover watery expanses which no man could hope to swim?) In his thirty odd years in Leavenworth and other jails, Bird Man wrote two books about birds and their diseases, "scholarly works" they have been called by those who ought to know. But on The Rock, no pets, no birds, not even a spider to tell your troubles to, and, anyway, total silence was the rule. Bird Man couldn't exchange so much as the time of day with Al Capone who was working in the laundry there.

As for Berkman, it so happened that the tunnel his friends were excavating from their end, under a nearby house, was discovered, and he was returned to solitary. That fact wouldn't be of much comfort to the Marie Laurencin girl or the black prisoner; nor was there any point in speaking of Berkman's computation of his future, which went:

---

* Ibid., page 373.

$$264 \times 30 = 7{,}920 \text{ days.}$$
$$7{,}920 \times 24 = 190{,}080 \text{ hours.}$$
$$190{,}080 \times 60 = 11{,}404{,}800 \text{ minutes.}$$
$$11{,}404{,}800 \times 60 = 684{,}288{,}000 \text{ seconds. *}$$

That he came to the realization later that he had allowed only thirty days per month when the year consists of 365 days, and at times 366, wouldn't cheer them either. So he revised the multiplication and was aghast to find that he had closer to 700,000,000 seconds to pass in solitary. "This is from the hospital, *sub rosa*," Berkman wrote on July 10, 1901. "Just out of the strait-jacket after eight days. For over a year I was in the strictest solitary; for a long time mail and reading matter were denied me. I have no words to describe the horror of the last months." ** But it occurred to me that it would perhaps be better to tell my two cellmates not about men, but about other women, for that would come closer to touching their own lives. I would not complicate things by dwelling on what Martha Tranquilla had once said very quietly. It was after she had served her sentence at Terminal Island for refusing to pay income tax, inasmuch as she had considered herself exempt from taxation, for she had claimed all the children of Vietnam as her dependents. She was asked by a magazine to write on the subject of the treatment of women in prison, and she said she could not. In her experience, she said, women and men were treated with equal injustice in jail.

I could simply begin by saying that once upon a time there was a woman named Alice Paul, and when I was a little girl I saw her every now and then because my aunt drew the covers for the equal rights magazine called *The Suffragist*. Sometimes Alice Paul came to lunch at our house, and once my grandfather, a gracious-mannered descendent of the Donegal Boyles, a man with an astute, legal mind, was persuaded to come home for lunch one day in order to meet a "suffragette." That evening, my mother asked him what he thought

* Ibid., page 229.

** Ibid., page 409.

of this young woman who had degrees from Swarthmore, and the University of Pennsylvania, and who had done graduate studies in English universities, and gone to jail with the English suffragists.

"She wrote her doctor's thesis on the status of women," Mother told her father-in-law, speaking gently, so gently that you could scarcely hear her, yet everyone always heard what she had to say. "She wanted first hand experience about the position of women in industry," Mother said, "so she became a factory worker in England."

"Very interesting," my Grandfather Boyle commented.

"And then," Mother went on, "she became involved in the women's militant movement in England. How I wish you'd been there as her lawyer to plead her case!"

My grandfather shook his head and smiled his gracious smile.

"You know that my judgment of a woman doesn't depend on what she thinks or what she does," he said, "but on whether or not she has a kissable mouth. Alice Paul does not have that attribute," he said.

But that wouldn't have been of much interest to the Marie Laurencin girl or the black prisoner, who was perhaps about to go to a sterner jail where her heart and her pride would finally have to break. It would make more sense to tell them about an American prison, I thought, and something about Alice Paul when she came back to Washington. I wanted to say to my cellmates, and to the deputies, and to the little black girls who had left the imprint of their lips between the bars on the glass pane of the door, that it was a part of our history, our own personal history. But I never found the way to say it, except by rocking the girl and her unborn baby to sleep, sometimes in the afternoon, and sometimes at night. Women had picketed the White House, went the chapter and verse and the rhyme and reason of the lullaby, and group after group of them were arrested, Alice Paul among them, and some were given three months, and others were given seven months, for obstructing traffic. "I'm seven months pregnant," murmured the blue-veined girl in her sleep, and I said: "Keep him in there as long as you can, because once he's out his troubles will begin."

In England, where Robin Hood could have been charged with assault with a deadly weapon in Sherwood Forest, and where women had burned mailboxes and torn down parts of buildings, sentences like that weren't handed out, was all part of the lullaby I warbled softly to her; but when I came to the lyrics about the hunger strike and the forcible feeding in the Washington, D.C. prison, I thought I had better forget the rest. Suppose they got the idea of forcibly feeding the Marie Laurencin girl because she couldn't eat the cold oatmeal and the fried eggs that had turned to leather by the time they got as far as lock-up? She was asleep now, so whether I sang or not wouldn't make any difference, but I didn't get up from the side of her cot because that might have startled her awake. Instead, out of the file of my staggering memory, I took the folder marked "Women," and I found the crumpled, handwritten letter I wanted, and I smoothed the creases from it with my hand.

> "Alice Paul is in the psychopathic ward (it read). She dreaded forcible feeding frightfully, and I hate to think how she must be feeling. I had a nervous time of it, gasping a long time afterward, and my stomach rejecting during the process. I spent a bad, restless night, but otherwise I am all right. The poor soul who fed me got liberally besprinkled during the process. I heard myself making the most hideous sounds.... One feels so forsaken when one lies prone and people shove a pipe down one's stomach.... Don't let them tell you we take this well. Miss Paul vomits much. I do, too, except when I'm not nervous, as I have been every time against my will.... I don't imagine bathing one's food in tears very good for one.... We think of the coming feeding all day. It is horrible." *

Actually, it wasn't a letter at all. These words, and others like them, were written on tiny scraps of paper and smuggled out of the District jail, written by Rose Winslow to her husband, and to the women who still picketed the White House gates.

* *Jailed for Freedom*, by Doris Stevens, Schocken Books, N.Y., 1976, pages 189-190.

Now the black prisoner was gone, and the shallow breath of the sleeping girl was soft as a moth's wing on my hands as I sat on the cot beside her. So I took another folder out of the file of our past history, this one from a legal subdivision labelled "Men," and the statement I wanted was instantly there. "Immediately after the police court judge had pronounced his sentence of sixty days in the Occoquan workhouse on these 'first offenders,' on the alleged charge of a traffic violation," Dudley Field Malone's voice said quietly, "I offered to act as attorney on the appeal of the case." * He had then telephoned President Woodrow Wilson in the White House and asked that he be allowed to see him without delay. "I began by reminding the President," Malone said in the uncanny hush of lock-up, "that in the seven and a half years of our personal and political association we had never had a serious difference. He was good enough to say that my loyalty to him had been one of the happiest circumstances of his public career. But I told him I had come to place my resignation in his hands as I could not remain a member of any administration which dared to send women to prison for demanding national suffrage." ** The President had replied that the women had been unmolested at the White House gates for over five months, and he added that he had even gone so far as to instruct the head usher to invite the women in on cold days to warm themselves and have coffee.

"The manhandling of the women by the police was outrageous," Dudley Field Malone's words to the President continued, but now it was difficult to hear him because of the wild, sad keening that had begun to come from the black depths of The Hole, just a skip and a jump outside our door. It was either the crying of a woman who could bear no more, or else the anguish of a cat wailing for the love of her kind in the total imprisonment of night. Then almost at once a deputy's voice, that I didn't want the Marie Laurencin girl to hear, rang out in the hall, saying (as a college president of San Francisco

---

* Ibid., pages 158-159.
** Ibid., page 159.

State had once screamed out to students and faculty through the police bull-horn): "If it's tear-gas you want, then keep right on and you'll get it! You'll get it, if that's what you're asking for!"

After that, there was silence again, and Dudley Field Malone said quietly to President Woodrow Wilson that the entire trial of the imprisoned women, conducted before a judge of the President's appointing, had been a perversion of justice. And then the President spoke out in total incredulity. "Do you mean to tell me that you intend to resign, to repudiate me and my Administration, and sacrifice me for your views on this suffrage question?" * It was growing dark in lock-up now, and in another minute the deputy on duty might rap on the barred glass and gesture from the hall for us to turn the light on, or might put her key in the lock and step in and herself switch on the ailing, overhead bulb. But I kept on listening to Malone, and now he was saying: "You ask if I am going to sacrifice you. You sacrifice nothing by my resignation. But I lose much. I quit a political career. I give up a powerful office in my own state. I, who have no money, sacrifice a lucrative salary, and go back to revive my law practice.... But I cannot and I will not remain in office and see women thrown into jail because they demand their political freedom." **

Just before the deputy's key rapped sharply on the glass, Malone exhorted the President to comprehend the inevitable impatience and righteous indignation of the women of America who had, for over half a century, demonstrated peacefully for a political right. He was urging him to take action on the suffrage amendment when the deputy called out from the hall: "Lights on!" I got up carefully, carefully, from the cot, soft-footed as a cat in my out-sized sneakers, so as not to waken the girl. And Malone, too, got to his feet and said quietly: "I left the executive offices, and never saw him again." ***
After I had turned on the switch, and taken my towel and soap from the drawer of my night-table, I went to the lock-up shower, where

*   Ibid., page 160.
**   Ibid., page 161.
*** Ibid., page 162.

plywood nailed across the window took the place of sawed-through bars and broken glass. It was then, as I soaped myself up and down and back and forth under the strong, warm needles of water, that I felt the lump for the first time. It was very small. It was really nothing. When I dried myself, it was still there. By six-thirty in the morning, when the cart creaked up the hall with breakfast for one and all, it had not gone away.

That was the first morning the Marie Laurencin girl ate anything. Slowly, and with great delicacy, she swallowed two pieces of toast soaked lifeless in the liquid that was neither coffee nor tea.

"I had a good night's sleep," she said. "Maybe that's why. The baby likes the food all right. You ought to feel the way he's kicking!"

I said I was going to ask that the doctor come and have a look at both of us, saying this as briskly as if I only needed to walk across the wall-to-wall carpeting to where the princess courtesy phone was waiting for me to dial the seven digits with my elegantly varnished fingernail, and speak the syllables of his name.

"I'm really, once and for all, going to get everything straightened out for us," I said. Sometimes the pill nurse, with her little brown basket of aspirin and castor oil and a vitamin or two, came into lock-up, and sometimes she didn't, but as she walked up the hall that morning, I tapped on the window in the door, and she turned and came back, and took out her ring of keys. "We both really have to see the doctor," I said when she stood there in the room with us, her gingham smock purple and gold and fresh as a daisy, a charitable lady with a neat crown of greying braids worn high on her head. "It's urgent. It's quite urgent for both of us," I said, and she took two aspirin tablets from the vial of them in her basket, and handed me one, and then crossed the room and handed the other to the Marie Laurencin girl. "But we really want to see the doctor," I said, and she answered in a low voice, as she drew the white serviette over her basket again, that the doctor wouldn't be back that week. "Then my attorney. I want to call my attorney," I said, but she had already opened the door, her defense an aura of vagueness, a mild bewilderment, so that it seemed now she was not quite certain this was the way out. Once in the safety of the hall, she locked the door carefully again.

Then the last talk I was ever to have with the blue-veined girl took place. She asked me if I believed what some people said, that if you couldn't get on with your mother, then you would have trouble all your life getting on with other people. "I'm afraid of that happening between him and me," she was saying, speaking of the unborn baby, when the two deputies unlocked the door. It was perhaps a little after seven o'clock, and they had come to escort me to still another lock-up room. This one gave every promise of being the most interesting of them all. In the very center of it sat a bare, white toilet, slightly spattered inside and out with excrement. It was clear that whatever you did, you did it with your sister-prisoners either looking on or turning their heads the other way. Five women were sitting on their cots, and a sixth cot stood there empty, its sagging mattress waiting invitingly for me. The five women, three black, two white, seemed very lively, and greeted me with something like delight.

"The ladies' room convenience don't flush from here," one of them called out to me, and they all burst into laughter. "You use it, and then you yell your lungs out for a deputy to flush it from the hall."

As I put my towel, and my piece of soap, and my suicide-proof toothbrush in the night-table drawer, another of the women said:

"Welcome to the toughest lock-up on the premises. They done their very best out here, and they come up with this one. Sisters used to flood the place, holding down the handle of the john, so they changed the system. They just don't seem to have no faith in us."

It was a large black woman sitting on her cot who said to me: "You look likes you could write a letter for me, lady. I gotta write a letter to my public defender about a son-of-a-bitch that had my thirty dollars in his pocket when he dropped down dead right before my eyes in the Flamingo Bar."

But there wasn't the time to discuss past, or present, or future prison history in the brief interval before a deputy turned her key in the lock of the door, and motioned to me. Outside in the hall, she said:

"Your lawyer's here."

I wanted to make my appearance before Bob as a woman if not of great beauty, at least of dignity, but I didn't have a comb or any lipstick to aid and abet me. So with my grey dress hanging unevenly and my sneakers flapping, I followed the deputy humbly to where he waited in the visiting room. We put our arms tightly around each other, and I don't know whether I told him first that I had been in lock-up for five days and nights, or whether I mentioned the lump to him right away.

"You know, where ladies get lumps," I said, "the usual place."

"Lock-up?" Bob said eventually, and his quick, dark eyes went darker. "Let me see the lieutenant at once," he said to the deputy standing near the door, her key-ring swinging in her hand. But the lieutenant wasn't on duty yet; she was maybe getting the auburn bee-hive of her hair-do into shape, I thought, but I stood there, humble and modest, and did not speak. "Get my client to the county hospital within an hour," Bob said. "I'll be back to check on that." And he said to me: "I'm going to court now to report this to the judge." I didn't cry out to him then, "What if I were black or yellow or penniless and forgotten, Bob? What if no one came at seven-thirty in the morning to speak his piece for me?" But before he left he answered with bitterness the words I hadn't said. "I know," he said. "I know."

V

One of the differences between a policecar and a paddywagon is that you can see out of a policecar. When a policecar skims quietly along a freeway, you can see the landscape of America on one side, and the passing traffic on the other. On the left, I could see settlements of rusticated motels, and gas stations, and super-markets, and signs saying "Grub," or "Eats," or "Body Work," and swimming pools bright azure oblongs in the early morning sun. On the right, Greyhound buses swept past, the riders in them looking down, as an audience high in the gallery might look, at the spectacle of a woman in a grey dress travelling alone inside a wire-meshed cage. Once or twice I wanted to raise my hand and wave to the passersby, but rightly or wrongly I believed that every prisoner has a certain dignity to maintain, no matter how trifling the sentence the authorities may have chosen to mete out.

So I rode on with my dignity, a bulletproof plate of glass, strengthened with chicken wire, between me and the driver, thinking of freeways as the arteries of America. And if these were the arteries, I asked myself, then where was the heart from which these broad veins flowed? Recklessly, heedlessly, they poured from state to state, from prison to prison (as well as from picnic-ground to picnic-ground), wooing us, urging us on, all of us, with their passion and purpose, from the solitary confinements of our lives. But what the passion and the purpose were, and whether our escape was actually escape, I did not know.

At the desk of the county hospital, the deputy who had driven me told the clerk that she was from the Rehabilitation Center, and was bringing me in for examination for breast cancer, and it might have been a misdemeanor, or even a felony, of which she spoke.

"The patient's name?" asked the girl behind the counter, and the deputy said:

"You don't need a name. Just put down number 2362."

Photo by William Minschew

THOMAS SANCHEZ

THE REAL
COWBOYS AND INDIANS

A History Lesson of the Great American West

On February 27, 1973 a group of Oglala Sioux and American Indian Movement supporters "liberated" the village of Wounded Knee, South Dakota, which was immediately surrounded by United States Marshals and FBI manning armored personnel carriers, gunship helicopters and digging in with automatic weaponry. On May 8, after the death of two Indians and wounded on both sides there was a stand down of arms and evacuation of Wounded Knee. What you are about to read concerns the early days of this conflict which proved to be the first American civil war in over 100 years.

CRAZY HORSE PAGEANT
SEE THE WORLD'S LARGEST OUTDOOR PRODUCTION
THE CONQUEST OF THE WEST FROM
THE VIEWPOINT OF THE SIOUX

"What the hell is *that* ahead!"

"They only use it in summer, it's empty."

"Looks like a cavalry fort. Pull over, I want to read the sign."

"Listen Antelope Dreamer, or Dreamer, or whatever the Christ you call yourself, I can't stop now. We can't be late for the Government news conference in Pine Ridge."

"Come on Keith, one minute!"

Keith jerked the wheel, swerving the car off the highway to a dead stop, "Make it fast."

Dreamer jumped out and looked up at the sign nailed across the fort's gates. Photographs displayed what took place inside behind barred log walls. Plastic tepees in flame, Indians shooting Cavalry in the neck with shotguns, galloping Cavalry ramming rubber bayonets into backs of Indian women trying to protect their children.

43

TALK ABOUT MOVIES ON THE WIDE SCREEN: TALK ABOUT
CINEMASCOPE AND PANAVISION, THEY'RE JUST HOME
MOVIES AFTER YOU'VE SEEN CRAZY HORSE PAGEANT ON A
STAGE 1,320 FEET WIDE! STEREOPHONIC SOUND IS USED! A
LIGHTING SYSTEM VAST ENOUGH TO PROVIDE POWER FOR
A SMALL COMMUNITY. MORE PALEFACES ATTENDED EACH
PERFORMANCE OF THE CRAZY HORSE PAGEANT THAN
WERE INVOLVED IN THE ACTUAL BATTLE WHEN THE SIOUX
CHIEF CRAZY HORSE DEFEATED CUSTER. THE CRAZY HORSE
PAGEANT IS DIFFERENT FROM ANY INDIAN PAGEANT
EVER... THE GREAT SIOUX NATION WAS THE ONLY MILI-
TARY FORCE TO FIGHT THE U.S. ARMY TO A STANDSTILL.
MILITARY EXPERTS REGARD THE SIOUX AS THE FINEST
LIGHT CAVALRY IN THE WORLD AND THE VISIONARY
CRAZY HORSE WAS THE MOST SKILLED FIGHTER OF THEM
ALL. IT WAS CRAZY HORSE WHO FOUGHT GENERAL COOK
TO A STANDSTILL AND LED THE ATTACK ON GEN. GEORGE
ARMSTRONG CUSTER AND THE VAUNTED 7TH CAVALRY AT
THE LITTLE BIG HORN RIVER ON JUNE 25, 1876. IN 1877 CRAZY
HORSE WENT TO FORT ROBINSON TO NEGOTIATE FOR
BETTER CONDITIONS FOR HIS PEOPLE. BETRAYED, HE WAS
BAYONETED AND DIED IN HIS FATHER'S ARMS. HIS BODY
WAS TAKEN "BACK TO THESE WILD PLACES." HIS FINAL
RESTING PLACE WAS NEVER DISCOVERED. CRAZY HORSE
PREDICTED HOW HE WOULD BE KILLED, HIS SPIRIT WOULD
CIRCLE THE EARTH UNTIL REINCARNATED TO LEAD HIS
PEOPLE TO THEIR FINAL DESTINY OF OWNING THE RED-
MAN'S WORLD. MANY CAST MEMBERS ARE INDIANS OF THE
OGLALA SIOUX TRIBE WHICH IS THE TRIBE OF CRAZY
HORSE. THIS IS THEIR STORY. THEY WANT A PART IN ITS
TELLING. THE CRAZY HORSE PAGEANT IS THE HAPPIEST
MARRIAGE OF HISTORICAL ACCURACY WITH HIGH DRAMA
EVER DONE.

"Satisfied?" Keith kicked the accelerator pedal to the floor.

Dreamer shook his head in disbelief and slammed the car door behind him, "Satisfied Hollywood is the real history book of America."

The high hills following the deserted highway along the swift bends of the Fall River faded before them against the morning sun.

PINE RIDGE 39 MILES

Keith slowed at the sign, turning down the reservation road. In a meadow a painted cartoon Indian Chief waved his spear at a message glaring across a billboard:

WOUNDED KNEE MASSACRE NATIONAL HISTORIC SITE & TRADING POST. AUTHENTIC ARTS AND CRAFTS. MASS BURIAL GRAVE. INDIAN MUSEUM. 51 MILES ON BIG FOOT TRAIL

Two slashes of barbedwire fence on both sides of the potholed pavement guided the road straight over the curve of a brown hill, the whole distance of the plains fanned off the horizon, stretched and humped like a great herd of sleeping buffalo, the shortfurred winter grasses racing over their brown bodies. Keith followed a pickup into Pine Ridge, through its rear window three rifles were racked and a bumper sticker declared:

A COWBOY DOES IT ALL ALMOST,
A COWGIRL DOES ALL THE REST!

The town of Pine Ridge swelled up like a lost ship on waves of windblasted grass. The first structure Dreamer saw was a church with a painted greeting on it side:

JESUS ONLY CAN FORGIVE
YOUR SINS!!!

"This must be the only town in America with more churches than gas-stations," Dreamer looked out the window at the main street with one church after another; spaced between churches small rough wooded houses leaned against the wind. From the barrenness of front-yards children stared in silence, shielded behind battered pickups and chromeflaked cars dead between the headlights, engineless beneath rusted hoods.

"Savages and Christians, Dreamer. Big Business," Keith turned a quick corner and pulled up before another church. "Best to park here, always have a hell of a time trying to get into the Bureau of Indian Affairs lot across the street.

Dreamer got out before a boarded and empty church. Thick slabs of lumber were nailed across the front door, across windows with their glass scattered inside over the concrete floor cluttered with pews turned on their backs, legs broken off and heaped in corners piled high with battered chairs.

"AIM was using this church as a staging area," Keith peered through a slit in the boards, "when Wilson, the Tribal President, found out he had his Goon Squad do a job on it. The Goons can't wreck all the churches in this town though, the Christians have them outnumbered."

Dreamer knew he was being watched. He turned to face those watching his every move, arms winged at their sides as they peered through binoculars from behind sandbags stacked along the rooftop of the highwalled redbrick BIA building across the street. Resting on sandbags machine-gun eyes of thick barrelheads aimed down at a line of women shielded by signs stuck out before them in the dead winter grass.

DON'T PUSH US!!!
WE LAY DOWN OUR LIVES SO MARSHALS LAY DOWN YOUR GUNS!
I NEVER WANT TO LEAVE THIS COUNTRY;
ALL OF MY RELATIVES ARE IN THE GROUND AND WHEN
I FALL I'M GOING TO FALL HERE!!!

The cars in the street between Dreamer and the gunmen on the rooftop did not slow for the words of the women, passing people did not turn their heads to the guns, or the words slashed in red paint on the wall of cardboard held up as protection before the women.

"Let's cross," Keith led the way into the traffic. Families hunched in the windwhipped backs of pickups speeding by paid no attention from beneath hoods of blankets bunched around their bodies.

Dreamer stopped to read the womens' signs.

"Come on, let's get a move on," Keith pulled nervously at the clipped ends of his mustache.

A boy appeared before the women. He was not yet a man but his speared warrior stance threw a direct challange, the wind flapping a red ribbon tied around the broad crown of his black hat. In the shelter of his shadow sat an old woman, her hands hidden from the cold by gloves of thick white socks. One hand supported the sign OUR HEARTS ARE AT WOUNDED KNEE, the other held a small American flag taking the full force of the wind. Dreamer moved along the line, the eyes of the women hidden behind the glare of sunglasses. The eyes of the gunmen on the roof and the boy stayed with Dreamer as he moved down the line and stopped. A young girl in a yellow parka pulled tight to her chin kicked loose a chunk of dead lawn, the brown blades scattering into the street were so unlike the brown life in her eyes; she alone did not wear sunglasses. The sign at her side stood higher than her body, HOKA HEY! CRAZY HORSE WILL COME AGAIN ANOTHER DAY!!! Dreamer smiled into the eyes shining with strength to defeat all guns aimed at her. The girl did not smile back. Dreamer heard Keith's voice calling to him across the glaring lake of the parking lot cartops, "Goddamnit I'm not waiting *anymore!*"

WOUNDED KNEE OPEN TO PRESS!
CEASEFIRE!

Keith looked around the empty conference room in the Bureau of Indian Affairs building, the only indication anyone had been there was the thick chalk message scrawled on the blackboard before him.

"You see what you made me do by talking me into stopping at that cavalry fort Dreamer? You made me miss the Government's morning briefing. We didn't even get here in time to cop a fill from one of the other reporters. The Press has been kept out of Wounded Knee for days. Everyone's beat us back in. We'll be scooped!" Keith turned, running down the empty corridor toward the parking lot. "Come on Dreamer, com'on, get your act *together!*"

They drove quickly, past the squared-off pink block building of the SIOUX NATION SHOPPING CENTER, past the small diner announcing CRAZY HORSE CAFE; they passed a pickup load of young Indians shouting and shaking their fists. Ridges of pines swelled in the distance like green veins across waves of stub grass. They passed the butchered head of a poached deer and slowed for an isolated intersection. A sign in the shape of a human foot implored FOLLOW THE BIG FOOT TRAIL. Keith turned at the sign.

"What's that sign mean, Keith? Follow the Big Foot Trail?"

"A tourist gimmick to get people to follow the original trail of Chief Bigfoot's forced march to Wounded Knee, only this time it's the tourists who will be massacred at the Trading Post."

Small pinetrees nudged the edge of the road stretching up the sudden swell of hill to be cut off by three jeeps parked side by side surrounded by Federal Marshals in electric blue jumpsuits with rifles raised.

"Yah, we'll follow the Big Foot Trail alright." Dreamer rolled up his window and punched the lock.

"It's okay, they're just going to search us and the car. Just routine to see we're not smuggling in arms. No need to worry, we're Press."

"Good, then they won't mind my knife."

"Jesus Dreamer. You didn't tell me when I picked you up hitch-hiking you had a weapon."

"Well all five inches have been hanging off my belt for anybody to see. You don't think I'd go in here without something to defend myself do you? What if I couldn't get back out?"

"Cover the damn thing up. It's too late to throw you out now. If they find that thing on you they'll bust us both."

"A knife is a one-to-one self defense weapon, it doesn't cut much ice against a gun."

"You're no Pressman like you said. I covered the whole Vietnamese War without a weapon, and I came back *alive.*"

"You think because you were a newsman, you could trot around exempt because you were unarmed. Tell it to the people in straw huts who were being napalmed. If I had been your enemy I would have shot you just as fast if you were holding a camera as a gun. You newsmen think you're a neutral race because you go into battle unarmed. The people on the other side don't have the luxury to report their own death."

The blood pumping at Keith's temples jumped to his hand and he banged his fist on the steering wheel, "I knew you weren't a newsman. I could tell from the beginning." He stopped the car and rolled the window down to hear what the Marshal in the electric blue suit holding a gun at his face was saying.

"Get out!"

Dreamer stepped onto the blacktop, in every direction across the shallow ravines, parked high on the knolls, were blue station wagons with Marshals leaning against them, the sun spotting the length of their rifle barrels.

"Dreamer, he wants to see your identification." Keith turned to the Marshal and spread his own wallet open on the roof of the car. "I told you, Marshal, he's not with me. I just gave him a ride. As you can see by my Press Card I'm with UPI."

"You're clean. Now you," the Marshal pointed his gun at Dreamer.

Dreamer slid his wallet across the roof. The Marshal glanced at the Press Card and picture on the driver's license.

"How come there's no picture on the Press Card? You could be anybody."

"If I was anybody I wouldn't have a driver's license with photograph, which matches the name on the Press Card. My name isn't *anybody.*"

"How come he calls you Dreamer? That's not the name on either one of these cards."

"That's what I'm called by some." Dreamer saw his reflection on the hard green edge of the Marshal's sunglasses.

"Do you have any firearms in the car or on your person?"

"No."

"Nor do I, Marshal," Keith held his palms up to the sun. "I don't have a thing on me."

"Is this your vehicle?"

"No sir, it's a rent-a-car."

"Open the trunk. You, Dreamer, over to the side of the road."

Dreamer stood on the narrow dirt shoulder, keeping a hand in the leather pocket of his coat pressed down to cover the knife holster. Lined before him, on both sides of the road, were more men in blue, watching, rifles tucked in the elbow wings of their arms.

The Marshal ripped the rubber trunk mat up and patted around the spare tire. "OK. Go on through."

Keith drove slowly between the lines of gunmen, the long bills of their blue caps tilted over dark green holes of sunglasses; in the rearview mirror he could see two stationwagons stopped and surrounded by the men in electric blue. Pines alongside the road opened up, scattering down into ravines, exposing hilltops brilliant with patches of snow. The hills protected the sudden fragility of a shallow valley below. From the valley floor an abrupt knoll raised from its back a white church, the sharp steeple of its bell tower pointing to a Christian cross towering over a small town, dwarfing a tepee pitched on the roll of meadow below it.

"Who are *they?*"

"AIM Security."

A red flag waved from the top of two cars turned up on their burnt sides blocking the road. Behind the cars on the high fender of a tractor two Indians kept their rifles trained before them, red ribbons fluttered from their rifle barrels and black braids fell across heavy coats.

"Are you Press?"

"Yes, here's our identification," Keith took Dreamer's wallet and passed it out the window with his own to the Indian who appeared from behind the wall of burned cars.

The Indian turned his back. The words stenciled down his Army fatigue jacket declared AIM FOR A SOVEREIGN NATION. "Out of the car and put your hands on the roof." He searched Keith and handed back his wallet, "OK you're clear. Now you."

Dreamer placed his hands on the roof, noticing the rifles two Indians on the tractor aimed at him were scoped to sight deer.

"What's in the holster?"

"A knife."

"What's it for?"

"Defense."

"You'll need more than that where you're *going*." The Indian handed Dreamer his wallet. "You're clear." He waved to the two on the tractor and they lowered their rifles. His stern face broke into a brief smile, "Welcome to the Independent Oglala Sioux Nation."

GUILDERSLEEVE AND SON
WOUNDED KNEE TRADING POST
WOUNDED KNEE, S.D.

Keith pulled into the long line of cars and jeeps parked the length of a log Trading Post. The black and white *GUILDERSLEEVE AND SON* sign on the roof had another message pasted over it.

AIM

The three letters were formed by bright red bumper stickers, each declaring VISIT WOUNDED KNEE, SITE OF THE FAMOUS 1890 SIOUX MASSACRE AND BURIAL GROUNDS.

"Lock it Dreamer."

"Why lock it? We're not leaving anything in it."

Keith slammed Dreamer's door, jamming his key in and twisting the lock. "You think this is a picnic out here with a lot of idealists? A girl from Newsweek had her trunk broken into and all of her camera equipment stolen. Everything gets ripped off around here. See that coming up the road?" He pointed to a pickup spraypainted green and brown camouflage and caked with mud, red ribbons flew from rifle barrels held by five Indians squatting in the backbed. "That's part of what they call Wounded Knee Tank Squadron around here. Ask them where they got it and they'll say they *borrowed* it from a nearby rancher or farmer who doesn't see eye to eye with their tactics."

The pickup stopped before a pipe skeleton of stripped gas pumps. Only the numbers, whirling on the stand of exposed pipe, testified to what was sucked out of the ground once was measured and paid for in dollars and cents. A row of teenage girls leaning on the fence across the dirt road shook their black hair down shiny backs of black parkas, clapping and laughing as the numbers whirred and gas filled the pickup. The driver honked and sped off. Red and blue gas foamed down the back fender as the men waved their rifles in clenched fists, bouncing in the back of the pickup heading over the hill toward the church. The girls bumped against one another and giggled as they ran into the road and waved. The screendoor beneath the sign, HOSPITAL, opened from the small house behind the girls. An Indian boy on a crutch appeared in the doorway, passing slowly before the girls who fell silent, eyes on the red ribbon above the bandaged knee. The slamming of car doors broke through the gaze of the girls' admiration. The boy stopped, turning a serious face to running reporters, their cameras raised. The boy waited for his picture to be taken. The reporters ran by him, cameras clicking at the Indian who appeared in the doorway, a black tail of hair knifed from his black beret straight to a black ammunition belt holstering a gun.

"Banks, can you tell us what this is all about?"

"Mister Banks has the Government met your terms?"

"Why is the Press being allowed back in?"

"Is it true a truce has been agreed to by the Department of Interior and AIM?"

"Dennis, is this man one of the two wounded in the firefight night before last?"

Banks smiled at the intense woman trying to juggle an armload of note books while writing quickly into another notebook at the same time.

"Yes, Betty he is."

"In the knee, the first to be shot in Wounded Knee was shot in the *knee*," one of the girls pointed to the red ribbon. The boy took a few stiff steps.

"You can tell he's playing it for all the romance he can get," Banks winked, triggering giggles down the line of girls.

The boy turned on Banks, a sneer grew into a laugh from his face; he understood, at that moment only Banks, the head warrior, could humor his wounded situation. Four feet higher and the bullet would have gone through his head.

The screendoor slammed and Banks disappeared. The reporters looked up and down the dirt road, confused.

"Where is everybody?"

"What's going on out here?"

Before the yellow log walls of the Trading Post a man walked slowly, his head to the ground, a red ribbon dangling from his shiny rifle stock.

"Can you tell us where everybody *is?*"

The rifleman didn't look up to the reporters as he passed the spray of paint on the wall, OGLALA NATION!!!

"I know where everybody is," one of the girls poked another beside her and they all laughed.

"Where?"

"Up at the community hall where Russel Means and them AIM guys are holding a news conference."

"Who knows where the hall is?"

"I do."

"Betty says she does!"

Dreamer didn't see Keith among the reporters running back across the road. He was gone. Dreamer jumped in the back of a stationwagon next to Betty, close up she was younger than she first looked.

"We have to go up the road we came in on."

"OK Betty," the driver backed out from the line of cars; two more cars pulled out, staying right with him. "Betty, how come Banks knows you by name?" The driver caught her reflection in the rearview mirror.

"Because we were the first paper in Minneapolis to take AIM seriously. Couple of years ago newpapers only gave space to Black militants, thought every other minority protest group was a cheap reflection of the Black Revolution. We reported on AIM years before the New York Times knew AIM existed." Betty reshuffled six notebooks from the stack in her lap onto Dreamer's knees, flipping through pages of pencil scrawl, rearranging markers and paperclipping pages, "You don't mind if I use you as a desk do you?"

"I don't mind."

Betty's eyes searched through the curls of hair falling over her face, "Who are you? I don't remember you coming in with us from Pine Ridge this morning."

"Dreamer."

"Aren't we all Dreamers?" Betty's laughter filled the car. "This lady up front is from the French Press, out of Washington D.C.. This gentleman's with the Canadian Press. Hey, everybody, we have a Dreamer with us. Meet Dreamer."

"Good to meet you Dreamer."

"How do you do."

"Are you a halfbreed? You don't look like a reporter."

Dreamer shook the offered hands and took the business cards coming across the seat.

The French reporter stabbed a pencil into the grey bun of her hair, "I don't think people in France will understand what's happening out here. They are interested, but don't believe half the things going on. Who'd believe this man Wilson could be a Tribal President, responsible for the welfare of 12,000 people, and only have a high school education and worked as a plumber for fifteen years?"

"I don't know how things are in France, Mam," Dreamer grabbed one of Betty's notebooks sliding off his lap. "I'd rather have a plumber as a President over a politician any day. These people just have the wrong plumber."

"You know," the French reporter ignored Dreamer, staring through the dust of the side window. "I never knew there was such beauty out here. If it hadn't been for this uprising I would have spent a lifetime never knowing such a place existed. These plains, stretching into such unworldly tranquility. I can see why people have been fighting over it for centuries. Someday, when this is over, I might come back, get a little cabin on those gentle brown hills. I thought of getting a cabin in Pennsylvania Amish country. Maybe here I can have more peace. What do you think of that, Betty? Do you think I could have a little summer place out here?"

Betty didn't look up from the notebook she was writing in, "You would hate it honey."

"Hey! Are you the dude?"

The big red-bearded man banged on Dreamer's window before he could get out of the car.

"Tell me, are you the dude?"

Dreamer stepped into the crowd pushing and jamming in wild knots of reporters, television crews and Indians all the way up to the main door of the community hall on the crest of the hill.

"Am I the dude? That depends."

"Are you the dude from CBS?"

"No, I'm from . . ."

The man twisted, the red blanket of hair swaying down his back as he walked away.

Betty slammed her door, "That's Red Crow. Probably looking for his connection of videotape since he is filming this thing for AIM. Different news people supplied him film during the early days when the Press was allowed in. Since he's been cut off for awhile he's probably desperate for more film."

"Hey Brother!" A VW van with pine branches lashed over the roof so it couldn't be spotted by the Government gunship helicopters from the air honked its way into the crowd. "It's me, Eugene, the street-medic. We were hitch-hiking together through Nebraska! I got in last night. What took you so long, Dreamer?"

The television camera men circled the van, forcing people back to get a clear shot. A young Japanese cameraman bent down on one knee, a camera braced to his shoulder; then whirled and focused on the crowd opening for two fighting dogs. A black dog pinned a brown one in the dirt, his teeth striking through to the skull. The cheering crowd split itself completely open so everyone could stamp and holler for their sudden favorite.

"Let that brown dog up! That brown dog's an AIM dog!" Russel Means, sitting on the wooden rail before the hall, shouted again. "Help that dog out! AIM dogs don't lose!" Means threw his head back and laughed into the sky. The laughter went through the crowd as a boy ran forward and kicked the black dog straight into the cord of tail whipped up between his legs. The black dog yelped into the crowd.

"Russel knows when to make a fight fair!"

"Hey Means, you sure that was an AIM dog!"

"You sure that wasn't an FBI informer!"

"Fire!"

"Where is it?"

A car raced up the sloping road. Behind the sweep of the next hill with the high white bell tower of the church rose a stack of black smoke. The car cut through the crowd and Dennis Banks jumped out. Means and several Indians surrounded Banks, their heads bent to keep the words tight in the circle, each presenting to the crowd on their jacket's back a painted red fist clenched into the profile of an Indian.

The reporters moved in on the driver of Bank's car.

"Where's the fire?"

"Who started it?"

The driver turned the hard glare of his sunglasses out the window at the cameras. "Don't know who started it. Maybe one of Wilson's Goons to detract from the news conference. We'll get it out."

"What's burning?"

"The Trading Post."

The circle around Banks and Means broke, from it emerged an Indian showing weather in his face beyond his age; colored ribbons knotted in the black hair above a spray of feathers caught the same breeze going unnoticed through the grass.

"Leonard! Leonard Crow Dog! Turn this way!"

"Mister Crow Dog will you face the cameras!"

"Do you see this as a Holy War?"

Crow Dog disappeared inside the hall, with him Banks and Means. The television men ganged up to protect their equipment as they tried to shove through the crowd at the door.

Dreamer watched the rifleman at the corner of the building with a young boy. The man kept the rifle braced at his shoulder, never taking his eye from the deer-scope he sighted along into the blur of hills, his finger at the trigger. The rifle moved, moment to moment, slightly to the left. Then Dreamer saw him, another rifleman leaning against a tree in the distance; his body still as gray rocks scattered across the hills, sun hit his raised rifle and exposed his position. The Indian boy looked at Dreamer, the wide brim of his black hat throwing a dark shadow over his young face, "We have our own snipers."

"Who's the target?"

"No target this time. My father is keeping two AIM's sighted way out there who are coming in from patrol. The Feds open up on them and they get blown away."

Against the long aluminum wall of a house trailer a Black man moved nervously toward the hall. His thin body seemed frail beneath the sharp creases of his khaki military jacket. His shiny loafers scraped the gravel noisily, as if unaccustomed to walking on anything but a city street. The black shield of his sunglasses reflected a column of smoke rising behind the white steeple in the far distance.

Dreamer realized most of the eyes he tried to meet were shielded by dark glasses. His own eyes were exposed. He followed the man silently into the bright light of the hall.

"The Justice Department will protect Indians from Wilson and his goons!" Means jumped from the table television cameras focused on through the brilliant lights. Banks took his place.

"Justice is taking down road blockades and pulling out! Justice terms are a total surrender, they know now American Indians won't tolerate any more abuse! We're going to win this war at Wounded

Knee, but it is only the beginning!"

Means climbed back into the light, looking over the room of raised fists, "We won this battle!" His chest seemed to be taking in bursts of air from the sudden shouts of joy, puffing him up, swelling his red shirt with a gust of strength. "Now all of us have to sit down, figure out how we're going to win the *total war!* Our work has just begun. We have to meet with the Interior Department in about a week. We'll remain right here in Wounded Knee! We beat Justice! We still have to beat the Interior Department!"

Banks stepped back into the heat of the lights, "A hundred years ago we won most battles but lost the war! We have to get this work finished. We need more people to come to Wounded Knee to get the work done!"

Means' hand went up against the shouting, "Leonard Crow Dog! A prayer from Leonard Crow Dog!"

Crow Dog stood. Only whirring film inside television cameras supported on slumped shoulders of puff-faced men could be heard.

"At the Sweat Lodge we will give our thanks to the Great Mystery," Crow Dog's voice came low and filled with force.

Raised fists and rifles filled the air, releasing storming wings rising from a thundering drum surrounded by youth. Victorious faces chanted the full song of highest plains onto the backs of birds escaping from the hall to the winter sky.

"We won Brother! We won!"

The defiant locking of arms grew into bear hugs.

"We beat Justice! Justice is pulling out!"

Television men were pushing into the dance, cameras tottering on their shoulders as they shouted for space. The circle of dancing took in Banks and Means, fists punching the air around them and a man in a business suit, sunglasses cocked high in the long flow of his gray hair.

"Mister Kunstler will you look this way!"

"Attorney Kunstler, this camera!"

Kunstler's hand came half way up his chest, the camera lights flashing through the crowd; he looked away self-consciously from the cameras as he threw his clenched fist into the air with the others around him.

"Betty, wait!" Dreamer ran behind the stationwagon headed downhill from the hall, braking tires ripped dust into his face. He grabbed the thrown-open back door. "How come you ran out so fast? What's up?"

"Pine Ridge. The Government has called an important Press conference telling their side of it."

Dreamer jumped in next to Betty, her leg pressed against him and she smiled through her curls. Smoke from the Trading Post clouded across the sky as they passed the roadblock of overturned cars, a rifleman waving them by from the top of the tractor. Beyond the road was clear. The men in blue were gone.

"I can't get by here."

"What the hell is going on?"

"We're trying to get down the hall to the news conference. Let us through."

"Look lady, we're *all* trying to get through, stop shoving."

"What's holding everybody up?"

"Wilson."

"Let me through!"

"Goddamit lady," the man with a big yellow PRESS card hanging around his neck glared down at Betty. Stop jabbing me in the back!"

"Which one's Wilson?"

"That one," Betty pressed her thin body against the wall so Dreamer could see past her. Wilson's the one with a crew-cut in the blue parka."

"President Wilson, do you think the Government betrayed you?"

Wilson's brown eyes raised slowly to the reporter's question like a waking lizard just spotting a fly. His body remained slumped against the wall, the weight of his broad head collapsing until the thickness of his chin rested on front of his parka. "No Federal actions on this reservation have been taken without the request and approval of the

Oglala Sioux. Tribal Governments on reservations have been dealt a serious blow as a result of the Wounded Knee incident. The Federal Government in effect suspended Tribal operations. Negotiations between armed activists and the Federal Government were seldom cleared through the constitutionally elected leadership of the Tribe." Wilson's voice stopped suddenly, as if a tape recording had been clicked off.

Dreamer shouted a question in with the other reporters, "Isn't what you're saying contradictory to Interior's position of not wanting to interpose their Department in what is basically an Oglala Tribal political dispute? Interior hasn't agreed to the AIM demand the Tribal Constitution be suspended and free elections held."

Wilson's eyes went through the metal sticks of microphones poking around his face and found Dreamer, "AIM is *not* the Oglala Sioux people. AIM can't make demands on this reservation. We are now faced with fighting Indians from other parts of the Country. The same organization which has failed our Indian Brothers in the cities now means to maliciously destroy our Tribal Government."

"Mister President, what do you think accounts for AIM's ability to attract such a broad spectrum of vocal support throughout the Country?"

Wilson clicked his tongue as if he was turning on a new tape recording, "They have the support of hordes of sophisticated, professional activists, like radical lawyer William Kunstler, who have taken upon themselves to come and tell other people how to run their lives. This condescending attitude is no better than the Federal Government's attitude. Indians can now run their own lives."

"Is it true you have deputized a so-called Goon Squad who answers only to you for their actions?"

"What do you want for your people?"

"I want AIM to leave the reservation so our people can feel security in their homes, and our children may go back to school, so we can get on with the real fight for the dignity and rights of our people."

"Do you think the Press has been fair in its accounts of the struggle here?"

"The Whiteman's newspapers have been distorted. You closed your ears to all but the dissidents whose intent is to dissolve our Tribal Government and install their own leaders. Most of these leaders are not members of the Oglala Sioux Tribe." Wilson's lips quivered, as if he had something further to say. Then he remembered what it was. *"Nobody* from the outside is going to tell us what to *do."*

"Come on! Move it through. Move it down!"

The force of men holding television cameras over their heads behind Dreamer broke up the crowd around Wilson. Dreamer felt Betty hanging onto his belt as waves of bodies pushed them to the end of the hall into the conference room.

"Quiet! I said we can't continue this news conference under these circumstances." The man at the front table snapped his briefcase nervously, sweat jumping at his temples played down his cheeks onto the black collar of his suit. His face searched in the blinding lights as the coughs and shuffling of the quieting crowd gave way to tape recorders punching on. "Now, what was your question?"

"What I asked, Mr. Director of Information," a reporter standing on a chair behind the bank of television lights shouted past whirring cameras, "is who instigated the peace? You people at the Department of Justice or AIM?"

"I repeat, the peace initiative was instigated by all parties. Part of the agreement was AIM remove personnel and weapons from bunkers to assure an open town in Wounded Knee. A question in the back."

"How many arrests have been made so far?"

"Chief U.S. Marshal Wayne Colburn can answer that."

The Chief Marshal stood up next to the Director. His eyes stared straight into the cameras, his silver hair brilliant in the strong light, the electric blue suit shining, "Seventy arrested before two-thirty today. Cases against them are being processed. There are warrants of arrest for a number of AIM people at Wounded Knee. When they are processed these men will become fugitives from Justice. The FBI wanted the community open to investigate. They will pursue all cases vigorously. Tribal Police are free to go back in. BIA police and FBI agents will be going in, anyone found committing a Federal offense or carrying an illegal firearm will be arrested."

"How long has the FBI been on the reservation?"

"Four weeks, at the request of the Tribal Council."

"Why didn't you withdraw from Wounded Knee earlier?"

The Director rose back into the light, "Our overriding concern has been to do everything possible to avoid bloodshed. Last night it became clear there was no agreement. This was due to the constant increase in demands by the AIM leaders as each previous demand was agreed to by Government representatives. This brings us to the situation at present. We have concluded that it is undesirable to continue to maintain roadblocks. Many of our Law enforcement objectives have already been accomplished. All the hostages have been released. Offers have been made by the Indians occupying Wounded Knee to make restitution to the residents. We are sending in lawyers from the Civil Rights Division of the Department to ensure that the rights of all citizens are preserved."

"Weren't those offers of restitution made by the National Council of Churches?"

"We hope all persons in the area, residents and non-residents, Indians and non-Indians, will lay down their weapons and join together to resolve their problems through peaceful means."

"Chief Marshal, have there been others on this reservation engaged in the shooting besides AIM and some of the ranchers?"

"Yes, that has been confirmed."

"Who are those people?" Is it the John Birch Society?"

"There will be a Grand Jury Investigation. Agents manning the roadblocks and armored troop carriers have collected evidence to present to the Jury."

"Thank you gentlemen," the Director snapped his briefcase shut. "About sixty indictments against participants in the Wounded Knee seizure will be sought from the Federal Grand Jury convening in Rapid City. Thank you for your cooperation."

The intensity of television lights died. Reporters shoved around

Dreamer for positions to shout questions at Colburn walking down the aisle forced through the room by the men in blue.

"Mister Colburn, how many Marshals will be left to guard the BIA building?"

"Will the Armored Personnel troops stay on alert?"

"Do you consider your pullback from Wounded Knee a defeat for the Justice Department as the Indians claim?"

Colburn stopped, muscles stretching the tight blue of his uniform across heavy shoulders as he swung around to meet the questions. "The FBI and AIM both had decided unilaterally to withdraw blockades. It was a coincidence it happened at the same time."

"Is it true the FBI has arrested armed members of the John Birch Society trying to attack Wounded Knee on its own?"

Colburn ignored the question. "We have not been defeated at Wounded Knee. When the Justice Department finally comes into Wounded Knee it won't be to capitulate to AIM but to improve the condition of all Indians."

"Chief Marshal Colburn, if you deny the effectiveness of AIM, why do you declare, after a ten day takeover, the Government is suddenly prepared to improve conditions for all Indians; conditions that have existed for over two hundred years?"

Colburn looked through the blue wall of bodies, "Which one of you asked that?"

"I did."

"What's your name?"

The moment he gave his name Dreamer knew he entered the FBI's computer.

"Hey, you look like a Brother! Can you help us?"

A skinny man with blond hair tied in a knot at his waist blocked the BIA building's glass doors from the outside.

Dreamer pushed his way through, "Depends."

"We're with . . ." A girl with the blond man shouted, behind her semi-trucks loaded with Armored Personnel Carriers chained to their flatbeds roared past. " . . . AIM! I said AIM! We're from the Lawyer's Collective in Denver!"

"Can you help us get in here to BIA? These Marshals won't let us get a foot in the door," the blond man pointed through the thick glass to the armed men in blue.

"Doesn't AIM have anybody in there?"

"No, we thought we'd try," the girl glared at the glass doors like she could melt them.

"You mean AIM hasn't had anyone at these news conferences to report on the Government's public position?"

"Not that we know of," the girl rattled the door, inside the Marshals put their hands to their guns.

"This thing gets crazier every minute," Dreamer looked at the girl in disbelief, then at the nervous Marshals.

"What's going on in there?" The girl put her face to the glass, trying to see down the long hallway.

"You better look at this if you want to know," Dreamer handed over his notebook.

"Is this what they are actually *saying* in there?" The girl looked up from the notes.

"Those are the words right out of their mouths."

"Do you realize what this means?" The girl grabbed Dreamer's arm.

"It means half of what AIM said it had accomplished this afternoon it *hasn't*."

"AIM hasn't won a *thing*." The girl shoved the notes at Dreamer. "What AIM gets out of the deal is actually a return to the status quo, which means AIM is being left wide open to Wilson's Goons!"

"And a lot more," the blond looked in at the Marshals.

"This is terrible." The girl watched over Dreamer's shoulder as five Indians wound their way through the cars of the parkinglot. "The lifting of the blockade has been a trick to let Justice come in and start indicting people."

"You two better get out there and tell them."

"Look," the girl tightened her grip on Dreamer's arm. "You're the one to tell them. You're the one who was actually in there and can state exactly what is happening."

"Please come to Wounded Knee with us. We have a car."

The five Indians came up behind Dreamer.

The girl cupped a hand over her mouth, "Careful, they might be Goons."

Dreamer felt a heavy hand clamp on his shoulder and turned to look into a face rutted with dark cracks like the bottom of a dried out pond.

"Hey Chief, you come out here to save us?" The Indian tightened his grip on Dreamer's shoulder. "You from New York? They got lots of warriors in New York. HAH!" The Indian stuck the club of his hand against Dreamer's chest.

Dreamer hooked his thumb into the thumb of the hand before him and locked it.

"Hey, you shake hands like an Indian! You New York Indians are real smart."

"Smart, sure," another Indian tilted back on his worn cowboy boot heels and snorted, "but are they smart enough to help us out."

Dreamer let his thumb slip from the leader's insistent grasp, "I'm from California, barely smart enough to zipper my pants in the morning let alone help you men out with anything."

The Indians laughed. "We bet *you're* smart enough to help us *out!*"

"Chief," the Indian before Dreamer was shaking, but not from the wind cutting around his body, "I *know* California." The deep lines in his face ran around and caught hold of the corners of his mouth in a smile, "I was *in* California. I picked grapes with the wetbacks in those hot fields. I'm glad you come to help. The Negroes in California got his *civil rights*. I know, I worked with some of them picking peas and peaches. I got respect for them. I got respect for *how* they got their rights. Indians should be more like Negroes. Why don't you tell some of the Indians around here they ought to act more like Negroes? Negroes in California don't have to live like animals in an open air ghetto. They got their rights. Chief, you think you can help us out? We ran out of gas in Porcupine, walked all the way in here, don't have enough for a gallon of gas between us. You can help us out BIG with ten bucks for gas."

His words scattered around Dreamer, but not from the wind, the whiskey breath released each word painfully, as if there wouldn't be enough breath to bear out a complete thought.

"Here's a buck. That's enough for more than a gallon. A gallon will get you back home."

The Indian closed Dreamer's dollar in his fist," We thought you could be of *more* help Chief. We'll pay you back though."

"Yah!" One of the Indians cocked his face at Dreamer, his dark eyes staring straight into the sun without blinking. "We'll pay you back when we get our Black Hills money!" He laughed and walked away with the others.

The girl looked at Dreamer with contempt. "You know they don't have a car. They just wanted enough for a bottle."

"I know," Dreamer nodded his head in agreement.

"I don't think you did the right thing."

Dreamer watched the men dodge drunkenly between cars of the parkinglot and disappear, "Neither do they."

"What the hell . . .!" The blond man pushed them back from the carloads of Marshals racing up.

The Marshals popped trunklids of their cars, exposing stacks of guns and ammunition. Newspaper and camera men appeared running from all directions, shouting to get photographs of arms being unloaded.

"No pictures! Off limits to the Press," the Marshals backed the circling crowd off with bayonetted rifles.

"Look," the girl grabbed Dreamer's arm, pulling him away from the Marshals, "are you going out to Wounded Knee with us or not?"

Dreamer watched the Marshals unload a machine-gun, "First I make a phone call. Is there a phone around here?"

"Sure," the girl laughed. "Across the lot over by the BIA Police station. Will you *come?*"

"Yes."

Dreamer made his way through the cars to a concrete building with a big yellow and black sign: *POLICE.* Five men in brown cowboy hats stood before the slot of doorway in the wall, scoped deer rifles braced at their sides.

Dreamer called to a man locking his car, "Say brother, could you tell me where the pay phone is?"

The man looked up, his heavy mustache drooping as if it bore the weight of all the cameras slung around his neck. He fixed his stare on Dreamer as if he had just taken a picture of him, developed it, ripped it up and thrown it in the mud. He saw Dreamer's long hair, long leather hunting jacket, long holstered knife and the scarred hide of thick antelope moccasins. He walked away without a word. Across shining cartops one of the cowboy-hatted gunmen raised his rifle and sighted it on a National Guard helicopter, tracking its flight as he would a honker homing into a pond. Dreamer walked toward the gunman.

The gunman took his eye off the rifle-sight, "This is a restricted area!"

"I'm just looking for a phone!"

The gunman jerked a thumb over his shoulder toward a booth at the end of the building.

Dreamer walked down to the booth and slammed the door against the noise of the cars honking around him and the helicopters overhead, "Operator, this is long distance to Los Angeles!"

"I'm sorry sir, all circuits are temporarily in use. Would you care to hold?"

"Yes operator, I'll give you a chance to make certain the call is bugged."

"Sir?"

"I'll wait."

Across the street a young Indian made his way through the traffic, his body moving slowly but intently against the stiffness of a wooden leg.

"Operator?"

"We're trying sir."

The Indian banged on the phone-booth.

"Please deposit $1.50."

The Indian knocked his fist against the glass door.

"One more quarter please."

"Get the hell out of there! Come on goddamit. Get out of the booth," the Indian kicked the door open with his wooden leg. "Goddamit come out now!"

"Hold it! Just hold it till I finish this call!"

"Come out of there man! Are you crazy! We're parked across the street ready to run you into Knee. That lawyer is crazy to let you hang us all up. We can't risk hanging around here with all this *Heat.* They know our faces. The Goons know us. We've all been busted already. Didn't the lawyer tell you that? We've just been sprung from the Rapid City jail."

"Hello, this is Pacifica Radio Los Angeles."

"Yes, this is Dreamer in Pine Ridge."

"Right, we'll put you straight through to the newsroom just like yesterday."

"Come on man, hang that fucking phone up."

"Dreamer?"

"Yes, the Interior and Justice Departments have just finished a news conference on the heels of an AIM conference announcing the lifting of the blockade. The entire matter is complex, actually more dangerous than before. If you're ready I can feed you the information."

"Dreamer."

"Get the fuck out of there. The BIA are watching from the jail!"

"Dreamer, we sent one of our reporters to Pine Ridge. She should be there by now, or tonight. She might be interested in your notes."

"You don't want what I have?"

"No."

Dreamer hung up.

"OK, man. Let's get the hell out of this town," the Indian was already into the street holding his hand against the traffic. "That's them waiting in the stationwagon. I hope we can get out of here without being busted."

The blond pulled the stationwagon up and threw the door open. Dreamer saw four men stretched out beneath a blanket in the back, they didn't make a move until the domed silver water tank towering above the town declaring PINE RIDGE INDIAN VILLAGE disappeared over the hills as the car sped away.

"Goddamit," the Indian stretched his wooden leg across the middle seat as the others sat up behind him. "I've been busted once trying to get into Knee, I don't want that shit again."

Dreamer leaned across the seat and shook hands with the four in the back; they were all teenagers. He turned to the one with the wooden leg, who was the youngest of them all. "How were you busted?"

"Soon's I heard all this shit coming down in Knee I decided it was time to fight. Shit, didn't even know where Knee was. Hitchhiked here from Oklahoma, right into Pine Ridge. I asked which way to Knee, waited till night then started walking." He looked out the dusty window at the deceptive gentleness of the rolling hills. "So this is where I was walking, out over the goddamn hills, pitch black, but I could see flares in the distance being shot by the Feds over Knee. Feds got me before I had a chance to get them. Threw me in Rapid City jail, BIA jail was already full up. That's where I met these other dudes, this morning when some rich broad in Kansas City bailed us out."

"You walked all the way out here with that bad leg?"

"Hey look Honky," he turned an angry face at Dreamer. "I can kick your ass with just *one* leg."

"Did you have a gun?"

"Nothing, just come over the top of a hill and see what looked like this big tank sitting there, you know one of the APC things, surrounded by guys with rifles aimed at my face."

"We're glad you made it Brother," the blond smiled into the rearview mirror. "This is Karen and I'm Roger. What's your name?"

"Edgar."

Dreamer offered the young Indian his hand, "Dreamer's my name brother, good to meet you."

Edgar shook Dreamer's hand without enthusiasm, "Hey, that's a funny name. How'd you get that."

"It's off of Antelope Dreamer. The past seven years I spent writing a book about some mountains in California, what happened to them and the people who were the first to dream them. These people didn't have Chiefs. They had instead many who led in the different ways of survival. One led the hunt of the ducks. One of the fish. One of the rabbits. One was the Antelope Dreamer. He didn't seek his dreams. They came to him. Antelopes appeared walking through his dreams. In the morning he would tell the people of his dreams and ask them to follow him to see if what he dreamed was true."

"Were the antelope always there?"

"That answer is buried in the heart of the Sierra Nevada mountains. I think they were."

"How's that explain you?"

"One of those people, a Washo, pointed out to me where he himself had killed running animals. He said he had dreams of those animals, so their Spirits were still alive. He thought maybe going back and trying to dream up the mountains, its people and animals, the way they once were, and how the killing was brought against them, meant I was like the last Antelope Dreamers who dreamed of antelope filling the valleys long after they had all been killed."

"I don't know," Edgar scraped a fingernail over the cracked seat cover. "I don't know if I can agree with that. That's a pretty powerful thing. I mean, if you're not one of those people how can you dream what they did?"

"Years later I understood the Washo's words. He wanted me to know anyone can dream animals up, if he is strong enough in his respect for that animal. What happened is we have become afraid of our own dreams. We lost the power. Afraid to dream those around us, Red, White, Brown, Black or Yellow. Afraid to dream ourselves into another because we have been taught we are different. What he wanted me to know was if I stopped dreaming, if I stood back from my dreams of those mountains and the history they gave birth to, I would lose. I would lose the mountains, its people . . . myself. In the end he dreamed me."

"Hey, you're a writer, you seen this book?" Edgar pulled a thick brown book from his back pocket and held it up. The gaze of a young

warrior with a drawn bow gazed from the cover: BURY MY HEART
AT WOUNDED KNEE.

"I know it."

"I'm half way through it. First book I ever got half-way through."

"That book ends in the mass burial ground right up here where
we're going. Here's a book tells the other side of the story." The
cover of the paperback Dreamer took from his coat was ripped,
yellowing scotchtape ran up the spine. "It's called INDIAN FIGHT-
ING ARMY. Want to hear a song from it that was written to
commemorate the slaughter of Wounded Knee and became a big hit
on the American Frontier?"

"Yah."

"This song was written for Custer's 7th Cavalry, which was at
Little Big Horn and Wounded Knee. The man who wrote it rode
with the 9th Cavalry Troop, which was all Black. It's called THE
INDIAN GHOST DANCE AND WAR.

'The Red Skins left their Agency, the soldiers left their Post,
All on the strength of an Indian tale about Messiah's ghost
Got up by savage chieftains to lead their tribes astray;
But Uncle Sam wouldn't have it so, for he ain't built that way.
They swore that this Messiah came to them in visions' sleep,
And promised to restore their game and Buffalos a heap,
So they must start a big ghost dance, then all would join their band,
And may be so we lead the way into the great Bad Land.
They claimed the shirt Messiah gave, no bullet could go through,
But when the soldiers fired at them they saw this was not true.
The Medicine man supplied them with their great Messiah's grace,
And he, too, pulled his freight and swore the 7th hard to face.
The 9th marched out with splendid cheer the Bad Lands to explo'e
With Colonel Henry at their head they never fear the foe;
So on they rode from Xmas eve 'til dawn of Xmas day;
The Red Skins heard the 9th was near and fled in great dismay;
The 7th is of courage bold, both officers and men,
But bad luck seems to follow them and twice has took them in;

They came in contact with Big Foot's warriors in their fierce might
This chief made sure he had a chance of vantage in the flight.'"

"That's disgusting. I didn't know the Cavalry had the nerve to glorify their slaughter in song," Karen rolled down the window and spat into the wind.

"That's the last time it'll happen," Edgar slapped the seat. "This time they won't get the chance to massacre a bunch of starving people. This time we'll kick their ass. What's that ahead?"

The burnt-out cars blocking the road caught the tilt of the lowered sun, flashing a gold streak across black pavement pointing down the valley to the white church rising from its center.

The Indian riflemen waved them to a stop, looking into the car. "Hey Brothers! Welcome to Wounded Knee!"

"Let me out." Edgar banged on his door handle, shoving the door open and himself out with it, grabbing the closest rifleman and bearhugging him until his hat whipped off and skidded on the pavement. "So this is what I've been trying to get to. Heeeryaw Shit!" He cut across the road onto the brown back of sloping hill heading toward the white church. "Here we come, *more* Warriors of Wounded Knee!"

Roger drove down the hill and parked in front of the Trading Post. The metal sign DON'T FORGET TO VISIT THE WOUNDED KNEE BURIAL GROUNDS hung by one nail above the swinging door fanning the stench of water doused charred wood into the air. "Hey, you know if any of the AIM leaders are in there," Roger's words stopped a girl in the flow of people going through the smoking doorway.

"No, I think them guys are over in the hospital house."

Roger led the way across the dirt road. Inside the house cartons of packaged and canned foods were stacked high around walls. People sat in every available space, not looking up from plates of food in their laps.

"You know where AIM is?"

A woman came from the kitchen wiping white flour onto her apron, "We're all AIM here."

"I'm looking for the *leaders*."

"I think Dennis and them are up at the tepee or Sweat Lodge with Crow Dog."

One of the eaters looked up, his mouth full of beans, "Russel's next door."

The door of the next house was already open, laughter filling the kitchen, its wall also hidden behind mounds of canned and dehydrated foods.

"I'm looking for the AIM leaders," Roger stepped into the room. "I've got a guy here who just came from the Press Conference at BIA."

"We're all AIM leaders," one of the men at the table tipped himself back on his chair. "Who are you?"

"I'm from the Lawyers Collective."

The man sliced the cake on the plate before him and wadded the whole hunk into his mouth, hooking a thumb over his shoulder as those around him laughed, "I think what *you're* looking for is back there."

Means sat deep in the sofa, a plate of food balanced on his knees rocking as one of the twenty other people sitting around him got up.

"Russel, I'm Roger from the Law Collective."

"Sure, I remember."

"We have something important."

"How important?"

"We've got a guy who just came from the Government press conference."

"So who cares what lies those guys say on television. Now everybody will see our side too. We had the news guys all around here today."

"This is something else, the fact is it doesn't square with the conditions negotiated."

"Wait a minute, I think he's ready, Means interrupted. "Yah, he's ready. Hey you guys, Red Crow is ready with the movie!"

A small video screen flickered in the corner, Red Crow stood up, his head bumping against the ceiling, "The quality isn't going to be too good. This is the best I can do."

"Hey you guys, shut up. We've got the *real* Cowboys and Indians movie here," Means winked at the people pushing into the packed room. "Shut up in the kitchen!"

Means was on the television screen, war cries around him joining the beating of drums every time he spoke of Indians standing up across America, of the need to set an example for young Indians, the need to claim the Spirit of a people never defeated on the battlefield. On the screen the black of his braid knifed at the side of his head, his face painted to War. He seemed giant, as if towering from the very ground soaked with the blood of those who had fallen before him nearly a hundred years before. Banks stood next to him, running through his eyes the stone current of a man prepared to battle his Spirit against whatever weapons were stacked against him. Bank's voice rose above the warwhoops to call into flesh the words of Crazy Horse, *"Today is a good day to die!"* The film title, THE ROAD TO CUSTER, declared where the action of Banks' words spoken in Rapid City would lead them all to, to a town where the man arrested for the stabbing death of Bad Heart Bull was on trial. CUSTER—THE TOWN WITH THE GUNSMOKE FLAVOR; the billboard on the road to Custer filled the screen; laughter around Dreamer filled the room as the smoke of Custer clouded the screen. Custer's broad main street wobbled in the view of a hand-held camera. Smoke poured from the courthouse where Means and Bad Heart Bull's mother were at the doors demanding entrance and a meeting with the Prosecuting Attorney. Glass from cars parked along the street scattered in air, tire-jacks swung through windshields. Sirens and shouts poured from the soundtrack, policeclubs thudding and cracking on the courthouse steps. More glass hailed through the air, rocks smashing through courthouse windows. Policecar windshields splintered beneath the pointblank swing of two-by-four clubs. Indians ganged in the street, screaming behind rocks sailing toward the buildings around them. Drifting away from the Chamber of Commerce the smoke gave way to a sudden surge of flames rising through windows and streaking for the roof. A squad of police marched around the corner, long barrels of riot guns pointed before them. Half-way down the block an Indian with a red ribbon trailing from his hair appeared in the swirl of bodies, a rifle aimed back at the squad of police. The shouting blurred into one voice, "Come on! Come on Mothers! We're ready!" From the other end of the street hardhatted police moved against the rocks and bottles as the brilliant flash of a flare whirled toward the courthouse where the screams and clubbing continued.

The room was silent. Dreamer noticed something about Means he had not seen that afternoon in the glare of television lights. The noble face Means presented to the world, as proud proof the children of the high plains had grown once again to defiant manhood, was covered and gouged with scars and gashes. Means crossed his legs, the leather of his new cowboy boots cracking the silence.

"What they did to me at the courthouse was nothing compared to what they did to me later when they got me in jail. They really beat me up good. About five of them."

"Oh Russel," one of the girls kneeling on the floor slapped his leg. "You mens are always bragging so much!" The rest of the room joined her laughter. None laughed harder than Means.

People blocking the kitchen doorway moved back as Banks came between them. The laughter stopped. A woman brought a plate of food. Banks turned it away.

"The meeting over at the Trading Post is still going on."

The people waited for Banks to say more, he didn't, as if only he and Means were in the room. No one else spoke, except Means.

"There's a guy here, says he was at the BIA for the news conference."

Banks looked around the room.

"I brought him, Dennis. To tell you and Russel what they're saying over there, especially the FBI."

Banks' eyes went to Roger, "Who is this guy you brought?"

"Dreamer, from California. He's straight."

Banks' eyes were on Dreamer, bringing with them all other eyes in the room.

"What are *they* saying?"

Dreamer felt the silence in the room turn from curiosity to animosity. It was obvious from the expression on everyone's face, just by his *being* at the Government news conference he was not to be trusted. He didn't know if what he had to report would be turned against him in the end.

"Well, what are they saying, man," a voice shouted from the kitchen.

Dreamer read from his notes, "Chief U.S. Marshal Wayne Colburn stated there are warrants of arrest for a number of AIM members. When warrants are processed those people will become fugitives from Justice. Also, about sixty indictments against participants in the seizure of Wounded Knee will be sought in two days from a Federal Grand Jury. FBI agents and BIA Police will be coming into Wounded Knee. Anyone found committing a Federal offense or carrying an illegal firearm will be arrested. The FBI lifted the blockades to gain access to Wounded Knee for purposes of investigation and pursuing all cases vigorously."

Banks' eyes went off Dreamer to Means, "We've opened our roads up to *them!*"

Dreamer continued, "I told Colburn AIM announced the Justice Department would protect those inside Wounded Knee from Wilson's deputies and police. Colburn stated that Wilson's Tribal Police were free to enter Wounded Knee."

"It's a trick, Russel," Banks stared nervously at Means. "We've been tricked. I told you we couldn't trust *them*. I told you guys in the meeting this afternoon; the guns must stay in the *heart* of Wounded Knee." He waited to see if anyone would contest his words, then threw his right shoulder back like a fighter ready to deliver his knockout punch. "The Government wants a massacre here . . . let's give it to them."

No one spoke, knowing only Means could answer the challenge thrown down by Banks.

Means stiffened, "We've got to talk to Kunstler."

"Instead of pulling a surprise attack on us, they pull a surprise surrender. They wanted to open Wounded Knee so they can arrest us," the hatred in Banks' eyes filled the air.

"Nobody can leave here," Means jumped up. "The FBI has photographs of us all, they want to knock us off one by one. Either the White pig police will arrest us or the Goons will shoot us in the back. They can't beat us together, nobody leaves here. We've got to tell all these guys that."

"We've got to tell these guys we're going to cut the roads and protect this town. We've got to have a meeting. They just want to come in here and kill us all. OK, they want a massacre, let's give it to them." The challange of Bank's gaze passed over everyone in the room. He walked out with half the people following him.

"Repeat repeat repeat," Means stood to follow, looking back at the blackened screen on the television across the room. "That's history repeating itself, the FBI wants to disarm us and to convict us. This is the way they got Chief Big Foot 83 years ago, right here in the same place. Disarmed him, and killed him!"

Along the roads coming into Wounded Knee, leading to the top of the hill, honking carloads of people clapped and sang. This was their destination, what the television showed them for eleven days, the white church, pitched before it the white tepee and the humped back of Sweat Lodge, its frame of bent branches holding heat in the hollowed earth with blankets and skins. On a log before the Sacred Lodge seven men sat in silence, wrapped in blankets against sudden cold, steam rising the damp length of their shiny black hair.

"Hey, you seen Kunstler around here?" Roger shouted into one of the sandbagged trenches dug deep into the slope of the hill in front of the church.

"Who?"

"William Kunstler."

The boy in the trench shook his head and turned his eyes back to the rifle he was cleaning. Next to him his partner called up, "You mean that old white guy?"

"Yah, the white lawyer."

"I think I seen him further up the hill."

On top of the hill, behind sharp white walls of the Catholic Church, was a graveyard. Within strands of barbedwire a sign stood beside a concrete outline emphasizing a rectangle on the surface of earth. Scattered down the length of winter flattened weeds growing through concrete cracks the faded color of plastic flowers were anchored by stones.

WOUNDED KNEE HISTORICAL SITE
THE BATTLE OF WOUNDED KNEE

Chief Big Foot and his band of Sioux men, women and children were on their way to the "Cuny Table Flats" where Chief Red Cloud and about 2,000 faithful followers were gathered to celebrate the Ghost Dance ritual.

They traveled south through the Badlands, past Interior, Potatoe Creek, Kyle, camped on American Horse Creek, passed through Porcupine and traveled south toward Wounded Knee.

About five miles from Wounded Knee, near Porcupine, they were apprehended by a contingent of the 7th Cavalry and brought into Wounded Knee. Tired, hungry, cold, some sick, including Big Foot, they offered no resistance but willingly came into Wounded Knee and immediately set up their camps.

There was tension and restlessness throughout both camps. The appearance of armed troops could very well mean encounter, and such was far from the minds and plans of the Indians who had been subdued and ignominiously humbled on reservations, poorly fed, clothed and sheltered, and surrounded by the military.

It is said John Barley Corn was in evidence in the Cavalry camp; which alone is an assurance of restlessness, enough to electrify the air and set off over-anxious trigger fingers. Alone, Big Foot lay helpless and a prisoner in a trooper tent, leaving the Indians without their leader.

By accident or not, on that fateful morning of December 29, 1890, without order or command, a deadly rifle fire broke out beyond control of commanding officers.

From there on, between rifle and heavy hotchkiss one pound fire, no mercy was shown the Indians. Fire ceased when the targets were either down or flight had carried them beyond range.

A ghostly hush slowly crept over a field of the dead and dying. Only the mournful whine of a freezing north-wester, the chilling heartcry of a baby, still clinging to the breasts of its mother who was beyond hearing, for she, too, was numbered among the dead, were the only sounds to break the numbness of the spell.

Several hundred lay in death or dying, Twenty-nine Cavalrymen fell in their own cross-fire. The Indians, the dead now frozen stiff, were picked up like cord-wood, thrown into wagons and hauled away for burial. One hundred and twenty or more were stacked into a long mass grave, dug on the hillside spot in a churchyard where the hotchkiss guns were set for action.

Big Foot lay in frozen death along with his faithful followers and so was buried in the long grave.

Sprayed in red paint across the yellow words of the sign Dreamer read,

FUCK IT!

From the bell tower of the church hung the flag of the United States of America, upside down.

"Dreamer! Brother! What's shaking! It's me, Eugene, the street-medic."

"Eugene, have you seen Kunstler?" Dreamer called to the man in the green fatigue jacket trudging up the hill.

"Not since this afternoon at the news conference. Been busy getting this hospital shaped up. Got an operating table and we're teaching protection against a gas attack. Got enough gasmasks to outfit a platoon. Most of these people have never seen a gasmask, let alone used one. We're going to get gassed sooner or later, and CS gas is bad shit. Makes you feel like your skin is on fire and gets you to puking and your skin is so hot you'll damn near want to use your own vomit shooting ten feet out of your mouth to put the fire out. I know. I was in Chicago at the '68 Convention." The pale white of Eugene's face stood against the last rays of sun being knocked down by dark clouds tumbling over the hills. "We're not going to leave here until *all* the demands of the Oglala Sioux are met. We've got to prepare. Like Dennis Banks said, we're going to make this the largest single mass encampment in the world. Somebody said they heard it announced on the radio the Black comedian Dick Gregory has plans to raise ten million dollars to build a shrine for those Indians who died in the 1890 massacre here."

Karen pulled Dreamer's arm, "Come on, we've got to find Kunstler."

"Wait a minute Dreamer."

"What is it Eugene?"

"There's going to be a big meeting at the Trading Post tonight. Shouldn't miss it. I found out who you are. We went through the '60's without a writer talking our side of America. There are Brothers and Sisters coming here from all over. You've got to make the meeting, get it all down. This is history. We've got to organize the Brothers and Sisters coming in here who don't know where to connect. Hundreds are coming, going to be thousands. This Wounded Knee fight is all our fight. People from the Movement are coming from all over America to get behind it."

"No they aren't."

"What do you mean, they aren't?" Karen turned on Dreamer, the wind punching the hair around her face in wild lines.

"This time they aren't coming."

Karen leaned her face close to Dreamer, her lips tearing back over her teeth, "You *fuck!*"

"That's him!" Ralph shouted down the hill.

"Where?" Karen turned her back on Dreamer.

"Down by the tepee coming up the hill."

All that was left of the day struck a golden arm across the horizon above hills gone black behind the man working his way through people ringed around the heat of bonfires.

"Bill! Up here!"

"Mister Kunstler, over here in front of the church!"

Kunstler reached the top of the hill and looked back, lights of cars flashed on all roads coming into town, sun was gone, smoke from fires scattered through hills drifting white against the dark clouds.

"Bill, we have something important to tell you."

"I just came from Russel," Kunstler's shoulders slumped and he gasped for breath.

"This guy was at the FBI briefing this afternoon."

Kunstler turned back to the scene beneath him. "Russel has asked me to represent him. He wanted an answer."

Karen and Roger looked out at the fires and headlights and said nothing, caught in the gravity of Kunstler's gaze.

Dreamer knew Kunstler's answer. He had seen it in the last days of the '60s, when revolting against the Vietnam War in the streets of America had led into the courtrooms and a dead stop.

"I told Russel," the bonfires lit Kunstler's eyes, "I told him I will."

Karen and Roger turned back with smiles on their faces. Dreamer knew the issues would never be the same again.

"Bill, this man was at the Government briefing. I think you should listen to what he has to say," Roger spoke softly, embarrassed at turning the lawyer's thoughts from all the days in court that burned in the future like the fires on the horizon.

"Here, read my notes," Dreamer handed over his book.

Kunstler held Dreamer's notebook up to catch the glow off the distant fires.

"There are alot of tragic inconsistencies in there, Bill," Karen's face caught the illumination of the fires.

Kunstler handed the notebook back, "This is not important. It's going to be fought in the courts now."

The drums beat, carrying chanting voices to the ceiling of the Trading Post. A strong smell of smoke came through the dim light, Dreamer walked around the charred wood of a sudden drop into the depths of a basement boarded off from the main room. Hundreds of people sang and chanted across rubble that once was merchandise filling rows and rows of shelves now overturned and jumbled like a wreck of boxcars in the big room.

SIOUX
UP
RISING

Everywhere the message was sprayed in giant red letters. SIOUXUPRISING! A man danced by himself in one corner to the pulse of drums, a can of beer in one hand, the American flag wrapped upsidedown in a blanket around his leaping body.

"Dreamer!"

Dreamer looked into the crowd, trying to find the caller.

"Dreamer! Here!"

He saw her, clutching notebooks close to her breasts, laughing as she was not able to prevent several notebooks flying from her arms each time she was caught in the currents of the crowd and bumped in five directions at once. Dreamer pushed his way over and grabbed Betty around the waist, pulling her to the wall, he felt the heat coming from her body.

"Dreamer, I didn't know you'd come back," she leaned against him, the full redness of her lips softened from laughing. "I thought I was the only news-person left around this late. The others raced to Rapid City to fly out soon as the news conference ended. All planes were booked. There's one open early tomorrow morning but I don't know how to get into Pine Ridge. If I can get there I think I can get to Rapid."

"How much space is left on that plane Betty?"

"They had three seats when I called before coming back out here."

Dreamer took some of her notebooks and moved her toward the door until he was hit so hard in the back the books scattered from his hands. He turned into Eugene's laughing face.

"Sorry, somebody rammed me from behind! Where you going Dreamer? You can't leave yet, the Warriors are having a War meeting now. There's going to be a general meeting in here any minute."

"I'm going to Rapid."

"You can't leave Brother. We *need* you here. The more people from the outside the less chance the Government will try to come in and shoot up Indians. They aren't going to risk shooting Whites and a lot of women and children."

"You've got the lawyers planning the next battle."

"There's people coming from absolutely every state. Even the anti-war activist David Dellinger is coming here to work up a massive protest march 55 miles from Rapid City to the Four Presidents at Mount Rushmore. It's going to be as heavy as the '60's. You've got to stay and witness this!"

"Eugene, I'm not your boy."

Dreamer pushed until he and Betty were free of the Trading Post. The sudden darkness of the road gave way to the roar of a tractor, the spotted eyes of its lights weaving a wild trail, its engine strained under the load of four men waving rifles, whooping their encouragement at the machine to keep its lead on the spotted pony racing alongside with three bouncing boys on its back.

Dreamer waited until they raced into darkness. When he saw the next pair of lights shining toward him he jumped before them and held his hands up. The braking pickup skidded to a stop.

"Are you going or coming," Dreamer shouted through the driver's window at the family of five in the front seat.

"Where you headed?" the driver called through glass.

"Pine Ridge!"

"We're going to Oglala, we can take you!"

"Let the lady get in here with us," the woman next to the driver shouted. "You ride in the back. That lady would freeze back there, she don't have no coat."

Dreamer climbed up and leaned his back against the cab to block wind slapping in sharp cold gusts as the pickup rattled and whined, speeding over hills gone black, except for the quick steel outline of windmills perched in silent silhouette against clouds moving faster than the pickup.

CRAZY HORSE CAFE

The pickup stopped. Betty slammed the door, "Dreamer, you wait in the cafe."

Dreamer pulled the door of the cafe tight behind him against the wind blowing hard through the street.

"We're not open." The small woman behind the counter did not look up from her counting at the cash register.

"I don't want anything Mam, just to get out of the cold for a minute." Dreamer clapped his hands together to push the sting of blood back into his fingertips.

"You like some coffee?" The woman looked up and surprised him with a smile in her dark face. "I've got a half a cup left over. I would just reheat it in the morning anyway."

Dreamer sat on a stool as the woman poured the last of the coffee pot into his cup and propped both arms on the counter, resting her head in her hands. The strong brown of her eyes gave way to tired flesh around them.

"It's been so busy here the last few weeks. We usually don't get anybody this time of year. Now every day we have people lined up. Are you a newsman?"

"Sort of."

"I hope finally this is all over. Can you tell me, is it all over? We used to have such a nice town here, before. It was a quiet town, we had our bingo to go to. Why can't the world just let the people on this reservation be? I hope finally it is over and people leave us alone forever."

"Dreamer," Betty pushed the door open, "let's go!"

Outside in the wind another pickup waited. Dreamer got in beside Betty.

"Dreamer, this is Arthur, he said he would drive us."

"Howdy," Dreamer shook the driver's hand, he was not more than twenty, all he wore against the cold was a pair of pants and a white tee shirt.

"I told her ten bucks each, plus gas," the overhead light reflected off Arthur's puffy face.

"What do you think, Dreamer?" Betty winked at Dreamer, pleased with her bargaining.

"I think we don't have any choice."

"Good," Arthur started the engine. "I've got to drop by home and tell Mom and Dad where I'm going. They won't like it."

Arthur drove through the empty streets to a small house surrounded by junked cars under a dark swaying bare-limbed tree. He ran into the house, wind flapping up the wings of its tar-paper siding. Light from the open doorway fingered chrome and rust of the cars in the yard as Arthur made his way back through with a man running behind.

"I said you can't do it!"

Arthur slammed the pickup door and rolled down the window, "I'm going. I've already taken these peoples' money."

The man pointed back to the doorway, light shafted from behind a woman and children peering into darkness.

"What about *her?*"

"I'm going. I didn't even have to come by to tell you."

"Your Mother doesn't want you to go. It's too dangerous, son. You know these roads at night, who could be on them. Anything can happen, especially now. You know what they'll do to you if they catch you."

"Dad, if I can't get back tonight I'll stay with Aunt Fry in Rapid."

"You promise me that! You promise at least you won't try coming back alone!"

Arthur rolled up the window, the man ran into the dirt road behind the pickup, his face a red blur in the tail-lights.

"Under the seat Dreamer, reach under the seat," Arthur turned onto the open highway.

Dreamer felt a cold box under the seat and pulled it out.

"Good, give me one of them beers, take one for yourselves."

Dreamer popped a lid and handed a can to Betty.

"You have mine, I don't want one," she leaned her head against Dreamer's shoulder.

Dreamer passed the can to Arthur, "You think we'll have any trouble on this road?"

"Naw, look at the speedometer, 95. I just keep it there all the way until we're off the reservation. Nobody dare get in my way at this speed."

Chuckholes ribboned across the road banged the truck until it knocked the music on the radio into strains of static, then back to music again.

"Let me have another of those, will you Dreamer," Arthur pumped his window down letting cold wind rip the empty can from his hand.

"Sure, think I'll have another myself."

Arthur took the cold can and looked at Dreamer's face in the glow of radio light, "Hey, are you an AIM?"

"No. How about you?"

"Me!" Arthur drank down half the can and laughed. "No. But half my friends are. What's going on at this reservation is most middleaged people are for Wilson; the younger ones not so much, but they sympathize with AIM. A lot of it is personal, bad blood between Wilson and Russ Means. You know that Trail of Broken Treaties last year when Indians took over the BIA building in Washington?"

"Sure, made off with a pile of incriminating documents. The Government claims AIM did six million in damages."

"Russel, he was one of the ring leaders, lot of people out here liked what the Indians done. There was a big celebration dance planned when Russel got back but Wilson stopped Russel from coming onto the reservation, put the word out to his Goons. Russel was driving all around the reservation trying to figure a way in, finally came through Nebraska. Thing is, Russel's full blood, Wilson is a mixed. But Wilson controls jobs in Pine Ridge, the *only* jobs. Got his relatives in big money positions, some aren't *any* part Indian. Wilson's people say it doesn't mean anything for Russel to be full blood since he can't talk the Lakota language of the full blood. You ask Russel to say something in Lakota, all he can do is stand there and look Indian. Maybe that's why he's a AIM and I'm not. *Blood.* That's reason for alot of hostility. These old peoples go way back. Even Crazy Horse's aunt is out here. You ought to go talk to her, tell you about the old times. But it's bad this blood thing. I know, I'm a mix, not with White, but Mexican. Mom, she's blooded Oglala. Lot of people don't talk to Mom cause she didn't marry Indian. I don't like that kind of stuff. But this is my home. Maybe if I get a good job and a house, I can get my parents to move to Rapid City. Give me another one of those beers Dreamer. Boy am I hungry."

"I know a place to stop."

"There's nothing around here."

"Up ahead in Hot Springs."

"I don't have any money," Arthur burped and wiped his mouth.

"I do."

"Good. I'm starving."

PIZZA PUB

"There's a parking place right in front, pull in there."

"No!" Arthur wheeled the pickup around and parked with his back to the restaurant.

"Come on, let's go inside," Dreamer opened his door.

"You didn't say this was where you wanted to go!"

"Come on in Arthur and we'll have some beers while we're waiting for the pizza."

Arthur slipped down in the seat until his head was lower than Betty's shoulder, "I'm not going in there Dreamer. You heard about the murder of Raymond Yellow Thunder?"

"What does this place have to do with that?"

"The guys over from Gordon what did it sometimes used to hang out in there. They have a lot of friends in Hot Springs. Indians don't go in there."

Dreamer went inside the restaurant and waited for a pizza. Along the wallbench old men warmed themselves in the neon glow of a jukebox, sitting perfectly still, paying no attention to Dreamer. The room was empty and silent except for two teenage girls at a pool table, their feet gliding across the sawdust floor, their bodies bent, letting the poolsticks go quickly through slim fingers smacking balls across the table. One of the girls turned, looking over the heads of the old men to the silent jukebox as if she could suck music from it, her young breasts too small to ruin the loud effect of her sweatshirt painted like a yellow traffic sign: *YIELD*.

Dreamer took the boxed pizza and left. Arthur had the pickup idling in the middle of the street headed out of town. Dreamer sliced the pizza with his knife as Arthur put the pickup back in its ninety mile an hour trance.

"You know the killing of the old man, Yellow Thunder? They didn't tell it right in the papers. Those white guys from Gordon, what they did was beat Yellow Thunder up and threw him naked into an American Legion dance hall; forced him to do an Indian dance in front of everybody. They pissed on him and cut his balls off, then locked him in the trunk of a car for two days. Kill an Indian around here and people treat you like a war hero. That's why AIM marched on the Court House in Custer a couple of weeks before they took over Wounded Knee. The White guy who killed the Indian, Wesley Bad Heart Bull, was being tried in Custer. The White guy was only charged with second degree manslaughter and released on the kind of low bond a man gets for hitting his wife. There hasn't been one case where an Indian accused of murdering a White has ever been *allowed* bond, and not charged with *first* degree murder. Give me another beer there, this pizza is hot."

Dreamer hadn't eaten all day, the steaming pizza stripped the skin from the roof of his mouth as he gulped it down, each drink of cold beer stinging tears to his eyes, blurring the lights of Rapid City scattered in drifts across the distant hills. Betty was asleep against his shoulder.

"Where is it you want to go in Rapid?"

"I don't know, ask Betty." Dreamer nudged her softly until she opened her eyes.

"We'll go to Alex-Johnson Hotel," Betty murmered. "I'm sure we won't have any trouble getting in, everybody probably checked out this afternoon."

"You know," Arthur could see his reflection on the windshield and sat up as if he was about to deliver a speech to the U.N., "this Wounded Knee thing would be over in a day if the Government paid us for the Black Hills like they promised. The Black Hills are called the richest 100 miles square in America. We owned them. You Whites took 650 million dollars from the Homestake Mine alone. You'd think the Government would be smart to keep their part of the bargain and pay us Indians off. Just what they spent in Vietnam in one day would pay us off. You ever see that famous painting, 'Black Hills Gold'? Supposed to depict what'll happen if Indians get their Black Hills money. Shows Indians staggering around drunk with whiskey bottles. There's a saying among Indians when they borrow money from each other. They say, I'll pay you back with my Black Hills money. It's a joke. Means you'll never get the money back. Just like we never got the money, or the Black Hills, back. What we got was Badlands. Government likes to tell everybody our reservation is big as the state of Delaware. They don't say they put a gunnery range on the reservation covering one-sixth of the land. As if the Feds couldn't find another place for their gunnery range, have to whittle us down more. The Government don't make *mistakes*." Arthur rolled down his window, tossing out the pile of beer cans in his lap as he slowed for a stoplight. The Government never makes mistakes. Look at Mount Rushmore, where they put it. We know they won the war, they didn't have to carve their faces in our mountains to remind us of it everyday. Whites don't make mistakes. Banks and Means know that, those guys both face 120 years in jail apiece, they know the average life of an Indian is 40 years. So what the hell?"

"That's the hotel. Up there," Betty sat up, her voice no longer tired.

"That's right. That's the hotel up there," Arthur pulled over, his tires scraping along the curb to a stop. "Yah sure, that's *right*. This is your hotel."

"Thanks Arthur," Dreamer got out of the truck behind Betty.

"Yah sure, *thanks*."

"Look, Arthur," Betty walked around the truck and rested her hand on his arm cocked out the window. "Please don't try to drive back tonight."

"Yah sure, *please*."

"Just pull over someplace safe and sleep," Dreamer slammed the door, banging the truck like a tin drum.

"*Safe?*" The word came slow and sarcastic from Arthur's thick lips.

"Goodbye Arthur," Betty turned and walked into the hotel.

"Dreamer?"

"What?"

"Can you lend me five bucks?"

"Why not."

Arthur took the money, a smile coming to his face as a look of triumph jumped from his eyes. "I'll pay you back with my Black Hills money."

Dreamer watched Arthur until he rounded the corner and was gone.

"Where's the lady?"

A clerk came to the counter, dangled a key at Dreamer and winked, "She said she had to make some long distance telephone calls, for you to check in and wait for her by the elevator."

Dreamer leaned against the wall across from the elevator and closed his eyes. The old hotel was quiet except for the swish of the elevator going up and down, its automatic doors sucking open and closed, mindless to the fact there were no passengers. Dreamer opened his eyes, his sense of time was beginning to fade down the long hall. He went up to his room and phoned to confirm the first flight West in the morning. He called down to the desk and asked them to ring Betty's room.

"Hello?"

Dreamer heard her voice. Once, in Spain when he was desperate with a call across to America, he heard his own voice echoing back, coming off the ocean's floor, the full weight of the water's universe crushing everything familiar from his words until they crackled in a hollow metal chamber. Betty's voice was that distant.

"Hello. Who is it?"

"Dreamer."

"Dreamer?"

"I waited for you."

"It's too late now."

"For what?"

There was a long pause before he heard her last words and the phone went dead, "Sweet dreams . . ."

ERICA JONG

EAST-WEST BLUES:

A New Yorker Goes West

New York the center of the earth? For years I thought so. Born New Yorkers have that problem. And most of them never get over it. New York sits in its smog and smugness, priding itself on being cosmopolitan. We are the center of the news media, magazine publishing, book publishing and so, to some extent, we can impose our egocentricity on the rest of the country. But no one is fooled. New York is not America. The best thing a New York writer can do is to leave New York. At least for awhile.

Heresy! New York is culture, talk, stimulation, the jazz of frenzied ambition. Literary New York was once described by Hemingway as "a can of tapeworms feeding on each other," and who can improve on that definition? Everyone who writes anything you might want to read has lived here at one time or other or passes through occasionally—but bring them all together at a party and they eye each other hostilely, or trade stories about their book advances. A literary party seems to bring out the worst in everyone. You want to run screaming from "the best minds of your genera-tion." You'd rather read them than meet them. Whatever juice they possess does not flow under these circumstances. The gin flows;

everything else freezes. And the talk? Money, money is the theme. Go to a literary party and you will come away with the impression that writers are more venal than bankers. They are not. They are only poorer. Bankers talk about transcendental meditation; writers talk about money. This is only because the latter are so pressed for it whereas the former can afford to be spiritual. Spirituality is expensive. Especially in New York where only the rich can afford light, air, an apartment that faces something green. Leave New York and suddenly you can afford trees!

The environment does affect your head. New York is grey, stony, hemmed in by towers. You walk narrow corridors between the buildings, never see the sky. Not seeing the sky makes people mean. Not seeing the sky makes people competitive. So little space! So little air! No wonder writers in New York all want to kill each other. And lacking guns (or the courage to use them) they write reviews.

But head west and suddenly you can breathe. You can see the sky. Gas station attendants suddenly get friendly. Waitresses "hot up" your coffee. Telephone operators don't hang up on you and leave you stranded in a phone booth without a dime. With a car instead of a horse you can "light out for the territory" and conquer the world.

I'm not talking about the New York I knew as a kid, the silent, white New York of the Great Snow of 1947, the New York of double decker busses on Fifth Avenue, of striped awnings on the buildings in summer, of sprinklers filled with half naked toddlers in Central Park, of "air cooled" movie houses that looked like Turkish pavilions or Art Deco Emporiums, of old Irish bars on Columbus Avenue, of big Checker cabs (without Plexiglas partitions against the muggers), of the fabulous doll houses at the Museum of the City of New York and the mind-boggling bookstacks of the Forty Second Street Library.... I'm talking about what New York became as I grew older. Jungle drums in Central Park. Old people mugged for a five dollar bill. The subways solidly, menacingly black. And the dream of the melting pot becoming an armed camp.

Somedays, I love it still. I walk down Fifth Avenue in the Spring and I fairly skip to see so many different faces. Or I look at peoples' knees and laugh. Have you ever noticed the laughter of knees? Each knee a little face, smiling, frowning. There is so much anger and passion in New York! Almost every other place seems bland by comparison. Stockholm and London are beautiful, but they don't tempt me. Amsterdam does. There's enough insanity and diversity in Amsterdam to keep an ex-New Yorker happy. Paris tempts me, too—if only for the vistas and the cheeses. But still, as an American writer, I felt reborn as I discovered my own country. And at the age of 32 I fell in love with the West.

I had been west before and had understood nothing. At seventeen I saw L.A. (on the way to Japan) and all I remembered were palm trees and the swans at Bel Air Hotel. At twenty I saw the wine country and the redwoods and understood nothing. It was only when I was older, when I had written a novel and three books of poetry in New York (nourished by New York's curious bittersweet milk) that I came west and (this time) understood what it was all about.

First impressions of L.A. The air *soft*. The sun is visible everywhere. People move generously—as if they had been reading Walt Whitman. The sea keeps falling into itself, bluer and bluer as autumn approaches, the pelicans dive bomb into floating islands of seaweed; the phosphorescent red tides signal to the UFO's that here is a beach on which to land.

I never much liked Beverly Hills. It struck me as a branch of Disneyland. The grass like astroturf, the cars too new, the windows of the houses too vacant (like the marble eyes of statues). There are too many goddamned Mercedes and Rolls Royces. People should be reminded of dented fenders sometimes. But Malibu is another story. Oh I hear that it, like New York, is ruined. I know Malibuvians of the thirties who cannot bear to look at the condominiums sprouting. They sigh for naked beaches of their youth as I sigh for my "air cooled" Broadway movie palaces (all now supermarkets). But to me, hot from New York, running from a bad marriage, the media madness that follows a notorious book, and sudden frantic fame, Malibu was peace. If Cary Grant could stroll through the supermarket unbothered, so could I. And the ocean glittered *almost* every day.

Most New York writers who come to California get taken to a whirl of Hollywood parties, observe the various horrible customs to be observed there, and go home smugly certain that they have seen California, and found it just as detestable as it is reputed to be. That California certainly is. Imagine people who socialize only with people who can help them make money. Imagine little fish wooing medium size fishes wooing big fishes who, in turn, are wooing whales. A veritable foodchain, an eco-system composed entirely of parasites. But there is more to Southern California that that. There are also people.

Ordinary people. People who drive old cars. People who work. People who don't. Artists who live in warehouses. Writers who have more time to write because they are not fighting the city.

At first I feared Los Angeles. Like all chauvinistic New Yorkers, I believed the myth that you "fall asleep by the pool and wake up to find it's twenty years later." But that is hardly true. As the frantic outer stimulus subsides, your inner voices get louder. As the hassles of daily life subside, there is more time to work, not less. And gradually the rhythm of the ocean enters your writing.

But the West I fell in love with, finally, was not Los Angeles. I fell in love with the gold and ochre desert, with the deep mauve mountains, the blue and purple lake country of Nevada, the brown-gold of the coastal ranges, the eroding yellow clay cliffs over the Pacific. One of the odd things about moving west is that your priorities change. Social life becomes less important, nature more important. You need only a few good friends and all that sky. It is such a shift from the priorities of New York that it can hardly be *described* there, much less remembered for long when you are back. Your whole relationship to the world changes, becomes more elemental. You *need* less—less shopping, less frantic partying, less ambition—because there is so much beauty around you.

That is the principal reason the West is good for writers. The inner dialogue gets louder as the outer distractions fade. And nature resumes its proper proportions in one's life. Certainly this will never do for writers of gossip columns, theatre reviews, and the like. "What on earth do you find to *write* about in California?" one of them asked me incredulously, on my return to New York. If you have nothing inside you will surely be "bored" in the West. But even those who believe they have nothing inside may discover something when they listen to the ocean and the sky. The sound of the sea has the same effect on the mind as following one's breath in meditation. The new-found peace produces energy, not boredom. And the energy is astonishingly creative.

I found that my poetry changed when I lived by the Pacific. It became less self-consciously clever, less interested in verbal paradoxes, less apt to end with witty punch lines. To grow up in New York is to be deprived of nature—although one doesn't see it that way at the time. Central Park is nice enough for flying kites and walking dogs (provided it's broad daylight and there are thousands of people nearby) but the spirits of nature have utterly fled that place and the sounds are all the sounds of the city.

My first "nature poems" were about apples and onions and other objects to be found in the kitchen because in New York that was all the nature I had available to me. I'm not knocking apples and onions. One can certainly discover God (or the Muse) in an apple as well as in the roar of the ocean. As long as one trains the mind "To see the world in a grain of sand and eternity in a wild flower," one can discover poems in every object, every vista. But there is something to be said for reasserting one's connection with the rhythms and sounds of nature, and this became possible for me living near the Pacific. In the East, man dwarfs nature; in the West, nature dwarfs man. The experience is properly humbling for writers. It is hard to be arrogant confronting the Rocky Mountains or the Pacific Ocean. It is hard to forget one's place in the natural order, one's smallness, one's vulnerability. All all these things are an excellent tonic for the chronic hubris of the intellectual.

New York is an arrogant city—even geographically. All those enormous towers perched on that postage stamp of bedrock. A Greek friend who came to New York for the first time last year was appalled. "I predict the whole thing is going to implode," he said. And coming back from California, those were my sentiments too. Now I never walk the streets of New York without envisioning it after the apocalypse. The buildings toppled, street lamps rusted away, wild flowers growing up through the cement.

But geography is not the only reason for a New York writer to leave New York. It's an excellent antidote to New York's reputation-mania to live in a place unreached by *The New York Times* (or at least indifferent to its hegemony), a place where people browse in the supermarket for books, oblivious to reviews, a place where no one cares who is the current darling of the literary establishment.

New York writers sometimes forget that books are for readers, not critics, that every page one writes has the potential of giving *pleasure* to a reader, not argument to a reviewer. Outside New York, nobody cares much what critic has said what about what book. Someone browses at the paperback rack in the supermarket, takes home a book, meets the author without anyone else's praise or blame intervening. That is the sort of meeting between author and reader one hopes for, writes for—the random discovery of one's book in a supermarket, on a library shelf, on the shelf of a rented beach house. Leaving New York reminds one constantly of the possibility of such meetings. There is a whole country out there where nobody cares about New York gossip. Thank God.

Still, in the two years since I've become a regular between New York and L.A., I've been drawn into constant arguments about the relative merits of the two cities and have been regularly caught in the crossfire between die-hard Eastniks and Westniks about the relative merits of each place. The dialogue goes something like this:

Eastnik: Your brains fall out in California... all that sunshine!

Westnik: You're just too uptight to appreciate it...

Eastnik: Uptight! What you really mean is that we're not stoned all the time like you are.

Westnik: That's because you're scared to feel anything.

Eastnik: I suppose you equate feeling with taking your clothes off.

Westnik: There. That proves how uptight you are.

Eastnik: Well, at least I don't spend all my time buying health food and doing Yoga and getting high colonic enemas.

Westnik: And what *do* you do? Drink martinis and shop at Bloomingdale's, let yourself get flabby, eat red meat, live cooped in an apartment?

Eastnik: I actually converse with stimulating people. Nobody out here ever finishes a sentence. You're all so laid back it scares me.

Westnik: Relax, will you? You have nothing to fear but fear itself.

Eastnik: How witty. Did you think of that yourself or did you learn it at *est?*

Westnik: What's bugging you?

Eastnik: When's the next plane to New York?

At one time or another, I have played both those roles. I can still feel both in my bones. But, of course both are drastic oversimplifications, silly stereotypes—which have little to do with everyday life on the two coasts. The trouble is, I think, that the media has the power to create the illusion of fact, and the image of California is dominated by Hollywood's myth-making publicity apparatus while the image of New York is dominated by the national magazines and news networks. Hollywood does not represent California, and publishing does not represent New York, but because these two industries control the images that go out to the rest of the country and the world, they have the power to make it seem so. From reading, *New York Magazine* or *The Village Voice*, you'd think that nobody lived in California except film people and from listening to people in California, you'd think that New York's cultural world only existed for the purpose of putting down California and everything Californian. One thing both Eastniks and Westniks have in common is cultural paranoia.

I myself have certainly felt the paranoia, and it has sent me shuttling from coast to coast like a shuttlecock in a badminton game played on the court of the whole United States. In New York, I miss California. In California, I miss New York. The rhythms of the two places are so different that I find less culture shock from New York to Stockholm than from New York to L.A. But in one sense this is lucky: I *see* both places more clearly because of the constant commuting. I used to regard New York City as a natural environment. Now it seems not only unnatural but bizarre to me. People stacked on top of each other in glass boxes—how odd! I used to find California bizarre—especially the freeways (on which I always got lost). Now they seem less bizarre. And I have gone from being someone who hated to drive, to being someone who often gets her best ideas while driving, talks to herself, giggles, and sometimes even screams out loud in the lonely car.

That's another thing about the West; it makes you understand the American love affair with the automobile. In New York, a car is an encumbrance, an albatross; in the West, it is your Pegasus, your pal, your womb.

The love of cars! I came to it relatively late in life. Girls who grow up in Manhattan have no reason to learn to drive and thus become more phobic about driving with each passing year. I myself learned to drive in Europe, at the age of twenty-five, my tutor was a G.I. from Tennessee who gave the driving tests on the Army Base in Germany where I then lived. He charged me 50¢ an hour for the lessons and he taught me well. I learned on a Volkswagen Beetle with a stick shift and graduated from there to a Volvo sportscar. Having waited so long to learn to drive, I would not *dream* of driving an automatic when I was finally queen of the road. I shifted and downshifted, learned to drive in rain and sleet, learned to drive with one eye out for the insane German kamikazes who populated the autobahns and the other scanning the rearview mirror for those huge European double tractor trucks that always threatened to suck one into the vacuum created by their passing. After driving among mad Europeans for three years, American driving seemed like child's play—even driving in New York. But it was not until I got out West that I really learned to *love* a car, to feel it as an extension of my body, and to lust (as I had never lusted before) after gaudy pimpmobiles, classic sportscars, Excaliburs, even surfer vans.

In California your car becomes your second home; of *course* you want a nice one. With a telephone perhaps and a bar in back and a stereo (and maybe even a bed?). You can have a convertible and never have to put the top up, and what the sun does to your hair will look a lot better than bleach. I nearly bought a Cadillac convertible pimpmobile when I lived in Malibu. It was a great bargain, only six months old, in perfect condition, fire engine red, and it was offered to me for half its normal price by a friend in the classic car business. But I chickened out. And I chickened out for a very New York reason. "What poet drives a red Cadillac convertible?" I thought. "They'll all hate me back home." So I bought a sensible, practical compact thing that doesn't guzzle gas and will probably be undrivable in a year. I wasn't really ready to make the California commitment yet. If I move back, I'll buy a custom surfer van in shocking pink—and let the poets who scoff at me be damned!

In California, a car *is* poetry. And in the desert, even former radicals drive Mercedes-Benzes with telephones. Would Roy Rogers have skimped on Trigger? In the West, cars are no luxuries; cars surround your body the way your body surrounds your soul.

Which brings me to another point about the West versus the East—namely the West's great sympathy for things metaphysical as opposed to the East's absolute conviction that things material are the only things that exist. On my return to Manhattan from Malibu, numerous friends accused me of having become "a California nut" (merely because I consulted a spiritualist now and then, had given up meat, had begun studying Yoga, and went to every UFO cult meeting I could find). Is it the grandeur of nature or the softness of the air that produces such sympathies in California? Or is it something else? Some invisible extra element in the air? The proximity of the Pacific Ocean? The sense of being at the end of the continent and about to drop off. Or perhaps it has to do with the exhaustion of the Westward Dream. Having used up the continent, what's left but the stars? The old westering restlessness will not accept the finality of the Pacific coast. Next stop, the galaxy!

California does seem to produce the most curious combination of spiritualism and materialism. Here, in the part of the country containing the most sybarites per capita of any region, you will also find rampant spiritualism, genuine indifference to money cheek by jowl with the most frenzied passion for worldly goods to be found anywhere on this earth. I have seen mansions in California that make the palazzi of Venetian princes seem like dumps. I have seen agents living in splendor unmatched by European heads of state, film lawyers living like rajahs, television producers bathing more splendiferously than Roman Senators summering in Pompeii, semi-stars, demi-stars (and some who are not stars at all) soaking in marble tubs under mirrored ceilings while the intellectual elite of New York gaze up at their peeling ceilings and wish they could afford to move. Part of the New York animosity towards California is surely no more than that: envy. The rich in New York live like the poor in California.

Yet it is also possible to be a happy beachcomber in California. The sun is everywhere and the sun provides. Food is cheaper than in the East—and better. Artichokes grow as big as chandeliers, health foods bloom in every supermarket; being unemployed is a way of life. There is less shame attached to it than in the East, because two of the professions California is famous for (actors and screenwriters) suffer chronic unemployment. Hence unemployment is almost honorific, a badge of status, the mark of an artist.

For the genuinely rich, the styles of spending money are so different from one coast to another that we might as well be in different cultures (and we are). The East Coast rich play down their money. Old L.L. Bean parkas, bus travel on rainy days, ramshackle co-ops on Park Avenue with kitchens that need to be renovated. In California, the Jacuzzi, the heated swimming pool, the Mercedes and the Cuisinart are not luxuries but bare necessities of life. To be rich means to flaunt other things: a projection room, an Excalibur, suede walls blooming with Picassos and Chagalls. But even more astonishing to the New York greenhorn is the fact that many of the people who possess these things are not necessarily rich at all—only *seeming* to be. Or else they are trying to live up to the success they hope their next picture will bring.

Why is it possible to be happily poor or lavishly rich in California—while in New York both poor and rich belong to the same gray middle realm? It has to do with the weather. The weather in Southern California is so bountiful (and the vegetation in Northern California so lush) that one has the sense of inhabiting an earthly paradise. This both encourages great luxury and, paradoxically, makes it unnecessary. It all comes back ultimately to being able to see the sky.

I did not always appreciate the virtues of California. My first love (at seventeen) was a Californian and he tried valiantly to lure me West when I was twenty-two. I refused to go. I felt then that New York was literary culture and that my mind would wither up and die west of the Rockies. I wanted to see Europe, to write about Florentine paintings and Roman fountains and Venetian canals before I considered my own country. I had nothing but contempt for America at 22 and I always wanted to sail in the opposite direction. New York was okay because it wasn't really America. It was just an island on the way to Europe.

It was only when I had gobbled up Europe and grown sick of the way lit'ry New York had gobbled *me* up that I could go West and appreciate what I saw. Leathery-necked cowboys at truckstops in Nevada, East Villagers who had settled in Santa Fe and Albuquerque (and were selling Indian jewelry), Midwesterners who were now Blackjack dealers in Reno, all held fascination for me. I walked through Virginia City looking for the ghost of Mark Twain. I admired the clotted muscles on the beach at Venice, and loved the names of the sleazy massage parlors in West Hollywood. I fell in love with the grandeur of the redwoods and the funkiness of the bikers and surfers. This was America—the best of it and the worst of it, the shit and the sparkle, the friendly, generous people and the insane commercialism, the splendor of nature and the incredible eagerness to fuck it up for a few dollars, the garbage, the ugliness, the neon, the glorious ocean, the awe-inspiring mountains, the brilliant desert, the towering trees, the endangered birds.... Who could fail to be thrilled by such contrast? Who could fail to be moved by the sight of purity and corruption living together like an ill-matched couple (who will fight and fight but never split up)?

It took living in Europe for awhile to make me realize how American I was. And when I came back I had no illusions about the expatriate's life and I had far less contempt for America. I loved New York during the first few years I was beginning to publish poetry, loved the fact that I could go to ten poetry readings a week, that every poet in the world passed through sooner or later, that bookstores and libraries were so abundant, publishers so abundant, magazines so abundant. The pace of the city thrilled me, the writers I met fascinated me; I felt I was living at the center of the action, was part of it all, alive, full of beans, inspired. But all that changed after I'd published a notorious book. Suddenly I became the show rather than the spectator, and writing in New York became more and more difficult unless I was willing to utterly change my personality and become cold, aloof, and anti social. So I fled New York.

When I came back a year and a half later, having written more pages a day in California and Nevada than ever in New York, I came back chiefly to check out my paranoia, reclaim my roots, find out what I had been fleeing. I found the work rhythm I had established in the West stuck with me still. I stayed home more, went to parties scarcely at all, had learned to happily ignore the ringing of the telephone, did more exercise than ever before—but I found too that I missed nature more than I ever thought I would and that the plenitude of cement and the absence of the ocean left me feeling like a prisoner.

Ever since my return to New York I have been house-hunting, searching for the ideal place to live. But I fear I will never find it because the ideal place to live is a mythical Pacific beach within walking distance of Manhattan. I may spend a few more years shuttling back and forth—but I have the sense that there is a house fated for me somewhere and that like a lover, it will eventually claim me. Until it does, I will walk the streets of my native city, feeling like an exile, and I will continue to drive real estate agents crazy with my impossible demands. Recently I've gone house-hunting in the Berkshires, the Florida Keys, the suburbs of New York, the beaches of Cape Cod. But I have a sense that sooner or later I will submit to

the inevitable. New England may claim me for a few years; the Keys
may play for me with their ivory sands and their blue seas. But the
dust of the West keeps accumulating in the corners of my eyes. I clear
it away every morning but it reappears again every night. Mysteri-
ously, it accumulates while I dream.

HOUSE HUNTING, 1976

Looking for a home, America,
we have split & crisscrossed
you from your purple seashores
to your non-grip, non-slip
motel bathrooms,
from the casinos at Reno
to the crystalline shores of Lake Tahoe,
from the giant duck in Southhampton
(which is really an egg shop)
to the giant hotdog in L.A.
(which is really a hotdog stand)
to the giant artichoke in Castroville, CA.,
the heart of the artichoke
country,
& still we are homeless
this 1976.

America, we have met your brokers.
They are fiftyish ladies in hairnets,
or fiftyish ladies in blue & silver hair like mink coats
or flirty fiftyish ladies
getting blonder every winter.
They tout your federal brickwork
& your random hand-pegged floorboards.
Like witches, they advertise your gingerbread houses,
hour "high ranches," your split-levels,

your Victorians, your widows' walks,
your whaling towns
instead of wailing walls,
your Yankee New England spunk,
your hospitality, your tax rates,
your school systems,
with or without bussing
your friendly dogs
& philosophical cats.

America,
We have ridden through your canyons,
passes, dried-up rivers,
past your flooded quarries, through your eroded arroyos.
We have sighted UFO's on the beach
at Malibu
& swum from pool to pool
like any Cheever hero
& lusted in motels like any Updike Christian.

America,
the open road is closing,
& toll booths block the vista,
& even the toilets are pumped
with dimes as well as shit.
The fried clams on Cape Cod
are pressed from clam scraps.
The California carrot cake is rumored
to be made of soy,
the hamburgers have never seen a ham.

The dreaming towers of Gotham
are sunk in garbage,
the bedrock softens,
the buildings list like drunks,
the Thanksgiving balloons are all deflated,
the Christmas trees don't even pretend to be green.

But we love you, America,
& we'll keep on hunting.
The dreamhouse that we seek is just next door.
Switzerland is a heaven of chocolates
& tax breaks.
Barbados is sweet & black & taxfree.
Antigua is Britain by the sea.

But we're sticking around, America
for the next earthquake,
kissing the ground
for the next Fourth of July.
We love you, America
& we'll keep hunting.
There's a dreamhouse waiting for us somewhere
with blooming cherry trees
& a *FOR SALE* sign,
with picture windows facing the Pacific
& dormer windows facing the Atlantic,
with coconut palms & flaming maples,
with shifting sand dunes
& canyons blazing with mustard,
with rabbits & rattlesnakes & non-poisonous scorpions,
with racoons who rattle the garbage,
& meekly feeding deer who lap at salt licks,
& pheasants who hop across the lawn in two-steps,
with loving dogs & aloof, contemplative cats,
with heated swimming pool & sauna
& an earthquake-proof Jacuzzi,
with carpeted carport & bathrooms,
& plumbing so good it hums,
with neighbors who lend you organic sugar,
& mailmen who are often women,
with huge supermarkets selling wine & kneesocks,
mangoes, papayas, & dogfood in fifty flavors,
with nearby movie theatres playing Bergman & Fellini

without subtitles,
with resident symphony orchestras
down the block,
but no rockstars living right next door.

We know we'll find you someday
if not in this life America,
then in the next,
if not in this solar system
then in another.
We're ready to move, America,
We've called our unscrupulous mafia movers
who always break everything & demand to be paid in cash,
& we have our downpayment in hand.
We lust for a big fat mortgage.
We've pulled up our city roots
& we've packed our books, our banjo & our dog
in a bright red gypsy wagon
with low gas mileage.

All we need is the house,
all we need is the listing.
We're ready to move America,
but we don't know
where.

Photo by Mary Ellen Marks/Magnum

HENRY MILLER

A NATION OF LUNATICS

"Go on, my dear Americans, whip your horses to the utmost—open all your valves and let her go—swing, whirl with the rest—you will soon get under such momentum you can't stop if you would. Only make provision betimes, old States and new States, for several thousand insane asylums. You are in a fair way to create a whole nation of lunatics."

—WALT WHITMAN

From *A Magnificent Farce* by A. Edward Newton, The Atlantic Monthly Press, Boston, Mass., 1921

In two short centuries we are practically going down the drain. *Ausgespielt!* No one is going to mourn our passing, not even those we helped to survive. In the brief span of our history we managed to poison the world. We poisoned it with our ideas of progress, efficiency, mechanization. We made robots of our stalwart pioneers. We dehumanized the world we live in.

The rejects from the Old World could have been accepted as gods by the aborigines of this continent. But they quickly disillusioned them, quickly taught them to fear and hate us. (It was we white men who taught the Indians how to scalp the enemy!) We proceeded in the same ruthless fashion with our own kind, who happened to have different views about living. We suppressed the very wonderful Oneida Community and other religious communities. We robbed the Indians of their land and did our best to annihilate them. We never attempted to make retribution.

It seems as if we were conceived in violence and hatred, as if we were born to plunder, rape and murder. Our history books gloss over the cruelties and abominations, the immoral behavior of our leaders, the fact, to take a small example, that one of the greatest men we produced, Thomas Jefferson, had illegitimate children by a Negro slave of his. They were nearly all slave holders, these men who formed this great democracy of ours. They named it a republic and a democracy, but it never *was* and is not even one now. A few patrician, wealthy families control the government of these states. Even in Walt Whitman's day the land was rife with corruption. *Leaves of Grass* is a marvelous song of the self, but the prose works which followed are a thorough condemnation of American Society.

Once I saw in a store window a framed photo of all the Vice-Presidents we have had. It might have served as a rogues' gallery. Some of them looked like criminals, some looked feeble-minded, some like plain idiots. The Presidents haven't been much better, to tell the truth. To be sure, politicians and statesmen the world over have a dull or foxy look about them. Churchill was no exception.

Lincoln's name is revered, yet he, in my opinion, was largely responsible for the War between the States. It was in his power to avoid a confrontation between North and South. The Civil War, like most civil wars, was an atrocity from which the country has never fully recovered.

It was also a huge blunder, to put it mildly, to have entered the first World War. Look where the great enemy of mankind is today!

War, war... I remember since early childhood all of them, beginning with the Spanish-American war, the Russo-Japanese war, the Balkan wars—it goes on unremittingly. As Jean Giono said in *Refus d'Obéissance* (Refusal to Obey), capitalism feeds on war. It could not exist without war.

Today war is made by all parties, liberal, reactionary or what. Communists are just as murderous as capitalists or Fascists. Man seems born to kill. With this country leading, we have now taught the rest of the world to annihilate one another, *and* the fauna and flora also.

The adventure to the moon held the public's attention for a brief spell, but today the feeling is that it—the experiment—was to no good purpose. (The Pentagon will reap the benefits.) Soon there will be no need for uniforms and drills and rifle practice; we can stay in our seats wherever we are and manipulate the deadliest of forces. All out war from the rocking chair! No need of generals, admirals and their ilk. Each and every man, woman and child a potential bomb.

When I mentioned earlier that we were on our last legs I meant to include our imitators the world over. We will all go down together. Perhaps the primitives and a few species of wild beasts will survive the holocaust. *Then* perhaps we may see the emergence of a new humanity. Certainly we who at present make up society are incapable of righting the ship of state. Every progressive idea we put into execution sets us back that much further.

From earliest times we have had our gangsters, our assassins, our corrupt politicians. When was there ever a good, clean, happy time? To my recollection, never. As a boy I began hearing about Tammany Hall. As a boy I saw the police on horseback charging a harmless mob in Union Square, as if they were trained Cossacks. As a boy the "heroes" I heard about were Admiral Dewey (a nincompoop) and Teddy Roosevelt of San Juan Hill. I never heard of Emerson, Thoreau, Whitman. My own "hero" at that time was William Jennings Bryan, the silver-tongued orator. I knew of Sing Sing and Dannemora and Leavenworth and such like. The great story teller (sic) in my youth was O. Henry! No one spoke of the man who got him started as a writer, Al Jennings, who shared the same prison block with him at the Ohio State Penitentiary.

Public Libraries, book stores—there were none in the vicinity of my home. I had to wait until I was twenty-one and met Emma Goldman in San Diego before I knew there was such a word as culture. Thanks to her, I went straight from Mark Twain to Nietzsche.

Not only were the Vice-Presidents a bunch of imbeciles, nobodies, but most everyone in the country was. How many great writers, great painters, great composers have we produced over the centuries? Better try to name famous poltroons!

Recently we had the Watergate circus. To observe people's reactions, one would imagine our politicians never committed anything but trivial mistakes, never any *crimes*. We always behave as if we believe that evil can be eradicated once and for all.

When Lincoln issued the Emancipation Proclamation we thought we had put an end to slavery. We never imagined the Northern ghettos, with racial problems far worse than the South ever knew. In addition to black slaves we created *white* slaves—the slaves of the machine age. The Ku Klux Klan still exists. The Mafia also exists! We may not have pogroms but anti-Semitism flourishes just as strongly as ever.

Indeed, for all our talk of progress, we are just as narrow-minded, prejudiced, blood-thirsty as ever we were. Just to look at the military situation—the Pentagon!—is enough to give one the shivers. The last war—Vietnam—what foul doings! Tamerlane and Attila are nothing compared to our latter-day monsters armed with nuclear weapons, napalm, etc. If Hitler subsidized genocide, what about *us?* We have been practicing genocide from our very inception! Whoever disagrees with us, away with him! That goes for Indian, Negro, Mexican, anyone. And then there is the TV and the cinema. With them everything goes. Children grow up watching crime, watching murder, thievery, torture, everything imaginable that is foul, retarded, barbarous. All part of our beloved "progress." And we wonder why, as a nation, as a people, we are falling apart.

I ask myself seriously if there is any aspect of this American "civilization" which I can praise. I can find none. The prisons are dens of vice. The schools are seats of learning—what? Today the teacher is afraid of his pupils! Everyone is in fear of something, down to germs. One dare not go out for a walk alone and unarmed at night. Indeed, one is suspect if one walks the streets at night. (42nd Street and Broadway has become the sink-hole of the world, just as Hollywood and Vine is the ass-hole of the world.)

How true the Brazilian proverb—*Quando merda tiver valor pobre nasce sem cu*—(When shit becomes valuable the poor will be born without assholes)!

Today it is a commonplace to discuss venereal diseases and the drug culture. Children in their early teens give one another venereal disease. The percentage of those who have these diseases is enormous. Similarly with drugs and alcohol. A nation of addicts! Even grandma gets drunk!

When I was twenty-one I went to Washington, D.C. I wanted to see what Congress looked like in session. What did I see? First of all, the spittoon! *Everyone,* it seemed, was provided with this convenience. Everyone apparently used to chew tobacco. What a spectacle! Uneducated louts with their feet on the desk, taking a swig from the bottle, too drunk, many of them, to stand up and make an intelligent speech. "And these are our representatives!" I said to myself. "Pfui! They ought to be driven out, like the Gadarene swine!" (As a partial result I have never voted.) That was sixty years ago. The picture hasn't changed much, except for the spittoons. I believe they are now passé.

In my youth no one I knew used drugs. There were drug fiends, of course, but not in great numbers. Today even "respectable" members of society are on dope.

Abortions have always been practiced, of course, but today it's the *in* thing. Abortions and divorces—they run at about the same rate. Not that *I* give a damn about the failure of marriage. The only beautiful successful marriage I ever witnessed was between two middle-aged homosexuals. Aside from this illegal marriage every other I have been witness to proved a disaster. I have said it again and again—"Marriage means the death of Love." But we glorify it, with the aid of Billy Graham and his likes.

If you watch the news on TV, you notice immediately there is little differentiation made between one thing and another. After announcing an horrendous earthquake in some foreign country, one slides to some petty scandal, usually of a homosexual nature, in Great Britain or Germany, followed by tidbits like blowing up a prominent bank, massacring a village, catching smugglers in a big hashish or cocaine deal, plus some fresh delights on the antics of our Washington leaders. Everything is related with the same screwball expression, a mixture of blank idiocy and abysmal indifference.

Here is where our young are receiving their education. What they are learning in school is of no consequence, no help to them in their battle with the world. If there were an ounce of reality to this bloody educational system, they would first be taught the arts of war, then the manly arts, including boxing, wrestling, judo and karate. They would be taught to kill with a clear conscience and to read the Bible for pleasure. They would be taught how to drink and smoke, how to bugger one another in times of necessity, how to make and throw bombs in times of revolution, how to rape (defenseless girls, women, grandmothers). In short, how to survive in an age of barbarism such as ours. (Of what use to study *Ivanhoe* or *The Stones of Venice?*)

The people of our time are just as rowdy, bawdy, filthy and obnoxious as in Queen Elizabeth's day. But where are the Shakespeares, the Drakes, the Raleighs?

What of the theatre today? When one thinks of the Continent, or even parts of Asia, our theatre, our music is almost nil. Rock and roll is not music. The shows on Broadway, and off B'way are not great theatre. There is no theatre for the *people*. In Germany, to take but one foreign country, virtually every town has a theatre, opera and concerts subsidized by the government. We have plenty of money for bombers, submarines, warheads, for all that is destructive, but not for culture, not for education, or for relief of the poor. What a thing to say of the supposedly greatest country in the world that thousands of our poor are content to live on dog and cat food. I say thousands, but for all I know it may be millions.

And what about our noble police force, our supposed protectors? What crimes they are guilty of! What hatred and suspicion they inspire! *Corrupt* is hardly the word for it! And our heroes? You will have to search for them in the ranks of sport. At the moment it is Muhammad Ali. Tomorrow it may be a quarterback or a left-handed pitcher. We have had our heroes, but most of them have been assassinated or sent to the penitentiary. Many are silent heroes. It's dangerous to be an outstanding figure (for the good!) in a country where we have cultivated a breed of man known as the White Collar, Protestant Anglo-Saxon—a monster created by the times, a type who will stop at nothing to carry out his whims. Other countries have dictators and revolutionaries, equally capable of committing atrocious deeds. But it takes the American, that "100 percenter," to commit his misdeeds with such a bland countenance, such an openly hypocritical air. To look back upon Vietnam is to be filled with nausea. And there are people who talk of veterans as "heroes," God forbid.

Above all the confusion, all the double dealing, is the atmosphere of suspicion. One picks up the newspaper and sure enough there are the same stories as yesterday and the day before. Mayors of cities, governors of states, presidents of banks, even religious leaders are not above suspicion. The cream, so-called, of society is just as criminal-minded as the dregs. Children kill because they are bored. They do it for kicks, as they say. There are fewer and fewer murders of passion, and more and more in cold blood and for no reason. If ever there was a sick society this is one. To my mind we are worse than the Romans were in their day. In Roman times it was the emperors and the patricians who were pathological. Today in America it is the citizenry. No, worse, it includes children. It is the children who are frightening. Under what moon were they misbegotten?

All the professions have become corrupt. Whether one be a physician, a lawyer, a professor or a judge, he can be bought. Money talks. Money indeed is the only thing that talks. All the rest is mute. All the rest watch unblinkingly while one atrocity after another is perpetrated. To speak of the public is to speak of the unacknowledged Sphinx. It hears nothing, sees nothing, smells nothing, says nothing. And all the while it gives off a vile odor—not the odor of sanctity, as in ancient times, but the odor of neutrality, of indifference, of "Fuck You, Jack! Look out for yourself! Put your shit together!"

Don't think, as I pen these excoriating words, that I am unaware of what goes on in other countries, under the name of one ideology or another.

Here we boast of having a two-party system. In reality it is a system of pure chaos. Other countries are looked down upon because of their "chaotic" state of affairs. Yet, what could be more chaotic than our own? At the head of this chaos sits a man presumably elected by the people. Yet, ironically, to be elected he must be a millionaire. Think of it! Out of all the possible efficient or potentially efficient leaders of 200,000,000 people, we are permitted to choose between only two. One must be a Democrat and the other a Republican. An Independent stands no chance. And only that Democrat or that Republican stands a chance who is a "friend" not of the people but of the vested "interests." Millions of dollars are spent to elect a fool or knave—in any case, a willing puppet. And this is what is styled a democratic form of government. How much better a benevolent dictatorship!

A man must be slightly gaga to want to become President of the United States. If he is not assassinated he is so harassed, so overworked, that he emerges from his term of office, an older, sadder (but not necessarily wiser) man. In short, if he survives his life is shortened by twenty years. And, even if he wished to, he cannot right the ship of state. He is but a pawn in the hands of the various greedy, blood-sucking interests. One would think in such situations that revolution would be imminent. Not in America! Fat chance, as they say. No, for all their woes and misery, our people have been thoroughly brainwashed to accept and endure any conditions imposed on them. And if they do begin to murmur and protest, to voice their plaints, they are quickly disposed of by the police and militia. It is almost as bad as under the Czars. We have our own Cossacks, our own Gestapo, our own tyrants.

Pardoning Nixon caused somewhat of a scandal, but nothing more. A small minority feel that he should have been sent to the gas chamber or at least to the penitentiary. He certainly is unique not only for his ego, for his stubbornness, for his hypocrisy, but for what he got away with. In short, he got away with murder. We will probably never see another like him. If we do we will probably shoot him on the spot.

From the foregoing one might think there was or is nothing in this bloody land that I ever thought anything of. But, like any other shit, I too have my heroes, my idols. They form a rather motley group. Here are a few: John Brown of Harper's Ferry, Aguinaldo, the Filipino rebel who held out against America until his death a year or so ago, W. E. Burghardt Du Bois, who was a great influence in my life and who finally ended up in Ghana after serving a term in the penitentiary, Emma Goldman, the anarchist, who opened the whole world of culture to me, Elizabeth Gurley Flynn of the I W. W., Sacco and Vanzetti, Malcom X, Jack Johnson, Jack Dempsey, Charlie Chaplin, Martin Luther King, Louis (Satchmo) Armstrong, Charles Lindbergh, General Robert E. Lee, Laurel & Hardy. I also love the Rocky Mountains, the Great Smokies, the Blue Ridge Mountains, the Grand Canyon of Arizona, the State of Arkansas, the Hopi Indians, Joe Louis, Buffalo Bill, Thomas Jefferson, Bill Nye, the Burlesk, especially Minsky's on Second Avenue, New York, Frank Kramer, the champion (cyclist) sprinter, Pocahontas, the ferry boats, the horse-drawn fire engines, the Metropolitan Opera, the silent movies and most of the vaudeville stars. I adored Elsie Janis, Harpo Marx, Greta Garbo and a thousand others.

Not everybody and everything stank. There *were* men and women who were not bigots, not racists. There *were* public officials here and there—Eugene V. Debs, Justice Oliver Wendell Holmes—who actually believed in free speech and justice for all. But their name was not legion. It wasn't "the land of the free and the brave" which wretched emigrants dreamed of. (Even today the Ku Klux Klan still flourishes, as do the Nazis. Unthinkable, but true.) No, it wasn't a healthy society such as one finds in Bali and Tahiti. It wasn't even a good medieval society. It had possibilities but they were limited. It was never possessed of revolutionary fervor. (The nearest we ever came to revolution was during the I.W.W. period.)

Every wave of immigrants was subjected to ridicule and abuse. Our politicians always backed the wrong side—the Fascist dictators, the military Juntas. Our foreign policy has always been a disgrace. In the eyes of the man in the street there has never been any great difference between a Socialist and an Anarchist.

We would never dream of recommending to our teachers the works of Prince Kropotkin. A saintly figure like Eugene V. Debs is almost unknown to the youngsters of today. Our youngsters are totally uninterested in politics, and rightly so. Their heroes are football and basketball players, rock and roll maniacs, gangsters and the like. (Not an Al Capone—he was too human for their taste. The cold-blooded variety is more to their taste.)

Nothing could reveal more clearly the deadness of our society than the so-called revolt of the young. I say "so-called" revolt, because compared to the Gnostics of old these youngsters of ours are like babes in the wood. Their inspiration, or nourishment, is drugs and alcohol, or rock and roll. They are agin everything but make no determined effort to change things. Had they just a smatter of that deep rebellion which animated the Gnostics they could alter this society of ours overnight.

No matter what is afoot—for good or bad—it is soon nipped in the bud. What shocks us today becomes commonplace tomorrow. There are waves of assassination just as there are waves of fashion.

The greatest police force, the greatest gangsters, the greatest arsenal of weapons, the greatest crime rate, the greatest corruption, the biggest army of whores, the most modern prisons (and the worst!), the finest insane asylums, etc., etc. Always the first, the best, the greatest, the biggest, the mostest. Here superlatives have lost all value.

Along with the Mafia and the fifteen-year-olds who kill for kicks we have the Jesus freaks of one kind or another, the Mormons, the Seventh Day Adventists and what not. A wonderful mulligatawney. Our Secretary of State hops about like a pigeon trying to bring peace to the world while his associates in Congress sell arms to all comers and permit themselves to be humiliated and blackmailed by the oil countries. We are in danger of being strangled, not by those giant monsters, Russia and China, but by little countries who have what we need and who make us pay through the nose.

To interrupt for a moment. I must say a word or two about two idols of mine I forgot to mention earlier. One is Al Jennings, a one

time member of Jesse James' gang who in his teens was holding up
trains and stage coaches, who admitted to shooting (with his pistol)
over forty men—but "always in self-defense," who spent some years
in the Ohio Penitentiary where he became a boon companion of O.
Henry and got him to begin his literary career there in jail. Later in
life he wrote his one and only book, *Through the Shadows With O.
Henry*, a book far better than anything O. Henry ever wrote.
Perhaps I grew fond of him because after he had been given a full
pardon by President Theodore Roosevelt, after searching a long time
and finding that his companion in the penitentiary was now the
famous O. Henry (a pseudonym), after strolling arm in arm up and
down Broadway. Al Jennings, upon being introduced to one of O.
Henry's many acquaintances, would inevitably be asked where he
hailed from. Whereupon Jennings, cheerful as a pup, would
reply—"From the Ohio Penitentiary," much to O. Henry's dis-
comfit. Years later, when his book was translated into French by my
beloved Blaise Cendrars, when it came time to send him his royalties
check, Jennings was nowhere to be found. And so, this same Blaise
Cendrars decided to go to Hollywood, find Jennings and give him his
check. The long and short of it is that, after spending several months
in Hollywood and finding no trace of Jennings, Cendrars decided to
return to France. The night before he was to sail who should appear
at his door but Jennings himself. They spent the night drinking and
telling stories and on saying goodbye Jennings presented Cendrars
with the pistol with which he had killed his forty or more men. Said
Cendrars to me one day, when reminiscing, "Jennings was the third
great bandit to give me his gun as a souvenir."

The other idol, curiously enough, is also connected with Cendrars. He is none other than John Paul Jones, the hero of the War of
1812. It seems that Cendrars had spent ten years researching our
hero's life, with a view to writing a book about him, as he had of Al
Capone and others. And so it was that I learned of John Paul Jones'
visit to Russia and how he put the boots to the notorious Catherine of
Russia. Naturally I never came across this fact in our history books.
A hero like Jones could never fuck the Czarina of Russia! Unthink-

able. (Nor do history books tell how she met her death—fucked by a stallion, after having surrendered to every man in the guards who protected her.)

As for Benjamin Franklin, who represented us at Court in Paris, we usually pass things off by saying that he was quite a ladies' man, or some such euphemism. For some reason or other distinguished statesmen, ambassadors and their ilk are not supposed to fuck, unless it be with their own wives. (Which makes me think that one of the reasons we may have treated the Mormons so badly was because they had so many wives. We were envious of all that free love-making.)

I would never have known about Thomas Jefferson's amours (with his slaves) had I not seen photos of his progeny in a magazine at the home of a Negro friend. Strange thing was, my friend liked Jefferson better than Lincoln.

Speaking of mountains and rivers and canyons a while ago, I forgot to mention such exciting places as Harlem, Chinatown (New York) and the Slaughter Houses of Chicago. Or my visits to some of the famous prisons and penitentiaries that dot the land. Nor should I overlook the great dance halls, like the Savoy in Harlem and the Roseland on Broadway. Nor the great bands, the great musicians who made these places famous.

Just as the great composer Gustav Mahler is said to have urged his pupils to read Dostoievsky instead of struggling with harmony and counterpoint, so I would say that (if we could push the clock back) the best supplement to a college education would be an intimate knowledge of the dance halls and the burlesk. No matter how permissive we seemingly become the streak of Puritanism in us is ineradicable. We have freaks among us who would hide the sex of animals. God knows what would happen to their likes if they were obliged to witness (down on the farm) a bull mating with a cow in heat.

I mentioned a while back the "rogues' gallery" of Vice-Presidents. Their wives are even worse. Aside from Jacqueline Kennedy, the only other *President's* wife who was renowned for her charm and beauty was Dolly Madison. One wonders greatly how these people ever made love. One wonders if by some slip of the tongue they ever mentioned the crude names given the sexual organs. Can you imagine a little dialogue of this sort taking place between a president of our country and his legal wife?

He: Good morning, Jenny, how do you feel this morning? Would you like to rip off a quick one before I go to sign all those papers? I'm horny as hell.

She: Please, stop talking thay way—it's indecent. You make me blush.

He: What's wrong this time—the curse, a headache, or your hemorrhoids? A good fuck would cure you of all that nonsense.

She: Your language is abhorrent. I don't mind having intercourse occasionally, but in a polite, discreet way. After all, you are the President of the United States.

He: Fuck all that—lie down and open your legs. I'm going to give you a good fuck, whether you like it or not.

Is such a conversation unimaginable? If so, why? Because he is President and she is First Lady? Does that make them inhuman? If the Czarina of Russia, Holy Russia, could fuck every man in sight and finally end up with a stallion, why can't we conceive of our President and his wife doing like the rest of humanity? However, when you look at the mugs of these Presidents' wives you don't need to ask any questions. It's written plainly on their faces. For them fucking is outdated. One wonders how they ever came to have children. (They might just as well have hatched ducks or weasels.)

Our history books gloss over such intimate details. Even insanity is a tender subject. It took a long time before I knew of Lincoln's sad plight.

To me American history is one of the most boring. The one great event was the Civil War. Unfortunately the wrong side won out.

The one great virtue we do have is free speech. In no other country in the world could I say the things I have just been saying about my country. Nevertheless, this freedom is not one hundred percent, as is imagined. There are many, many ways of preventing the truth from coming out. And of squelching unwelcome views of a writer or thinker. Just as one "pays one's dues" to become a movie star, as they say, so a bold, fearless writer pays in one way or another. I paid by going hungry, by being censored, by waiting until I was sixty years old before I could open a bank account. The fact that under Hitler I might have been tortured and shot doesn't sweeten the pill. In a sense, censorship is with us always. The men in power know how to protect themselves. The man who got away with it, as I said earlier, was Nixon. And, to be honest, I see nothing to prevent another Nixon from arising tomorrow. We have not improved; politics is still the same dirty game it always was. Worst of all, or so it would seem, human beings don't change. A thousand Billy Grahams wouldn't alter things by a hair. Among occultists there seems to be a belief that if ever a fundamental change for the better occurs, it will be in America. I would like nothing better than for this to become the truth. Bitter and unpalatable as my words may sound, I do not hate America or even Americans. If I look upon our history as a total flop, I could say the same about most civilized countries. As I said somewhere I can think of no individual in any of the great countries of the world who can say, as do the Pygmies: "We are content as we are. We see no reason to change!" Indeed the very thought is unthinkable to civilized man. And of all the civilized peoples in the world I regard the American as the most restless, the most unsatisfied, the idiot who thinks he can change the world into his own image of it. In the process of making the world better, as he foolishly imagines, he is poisoning it, destroying it. Walt Whitman observed the process taking place over a hundred years ago. He referred to us as a nation of lunatics. Walt Whitman may well have been the greatest American who ever lived!

Here are Whitman's own words written about a hundred years ago: "Go on, my Dear Americans, whip your horses to the utmost—excitement! money! politics! Open all your valves and let her go—swing, whirl with the rest. You will soon get under such momentum you can't stop if you would. Only make provision betimes, old States, and new States, for several thousand insane asylums. You are in a fair way to create a whole nation of lunatics."

Finis

FOUR VISIONS OF AMERICA
WAS DESIGNED BY NOEL YOUNG,
SET IN JANSON BY CHARLENE McADAMS,
PRINTED & BOUND BY R.R. DONNELLEY & SONS
IN CRAWFORDSVILLE, INDIANA.
225 COPIES WERE NUMBERED & SIGNED
BY THE AUTHORS, MARCH 1977.

Macbeth: How now, you secret, black and midnight hags! What is it you do?

SHAKESPEARE FOR YOUNG PEOPLE

BOOK 4

MACBETH

FOR YOUNG PEOPLE

by
William Shakespeare

edited and illustrated by
Diane Davidson
music by Diane Davidson

SWAN BOOKS
FAIR OAKS, CALIFORNIA

Published by:

SWAN BOOKS

P.O. Box 2498

Fair Oaks, California 95628

Printed in the United States of America

Library of Congress Cataloging-in-Publication Data

Shakespeare, William, 1564–1616.
  Macbeth for young people.

  (Shakespeare for young people ; bk. 4)
  Summary: An abridged version of Shakespeare's
original text, with suggestions for simple staging.
Includes parenthetical explanations and descriptions
within the text and announcers who summarize deleted
passages.
    1. Children's plays, English. [1. Plays]
I. Davidson, Diane. II. Title. III. Series:
Shakespeare, William, 1564–1616. Shakespeare for
young people ; bk. 4.
PR2823.A25 1986   822.3'3   86–5955
ISBN 0-934048-21-5 (pbk.)

TO THE TEACHER OR PARENT

Young people can grow up loving Shakespeare if they act out his plays. Since Shakespeare wrote for the theater, not for the printed page, he is most exciting on his own ground.

Many people are afraid that the young will not understand Shakespeare's words. To help these actors follow the story, the editor has added two optional announcers, who introduce and explain scenes. However, young people pick up the general meaning with surprising ease, and they enjoy the words without completely understanding them at first. Their ears tell them the phrases often sound like music, and the plays are full of marvelous scenes.

After all, Shakespeare is not called the best of all writers because he is hard. He is the best of all writers because he is enjoyable!

HOW TO BEGIN

At first, students may find the script too difficult to enjoy, so one way to start is for the director to read the play aloud. Between scenes, he can ask, "What do you think is going to happen next?" or "Do you think the character should do this?" After the students become familiar with the story and words, they can try out for parts by reading different scenes. In the end, the director should pick the actors he thinks are best, emphasizing, "There are no small parts. Everybody helps in a production."

The plays can be presented in several ways.

In the simplest form, the students can read the script aloud, sitting in their seats. This will do well enough, but it is more fun to put on the actual show.

What can a director do to help his actors?

One main point in directing is to have the actors speak the words loudly and clearly. It helps if they speak a little

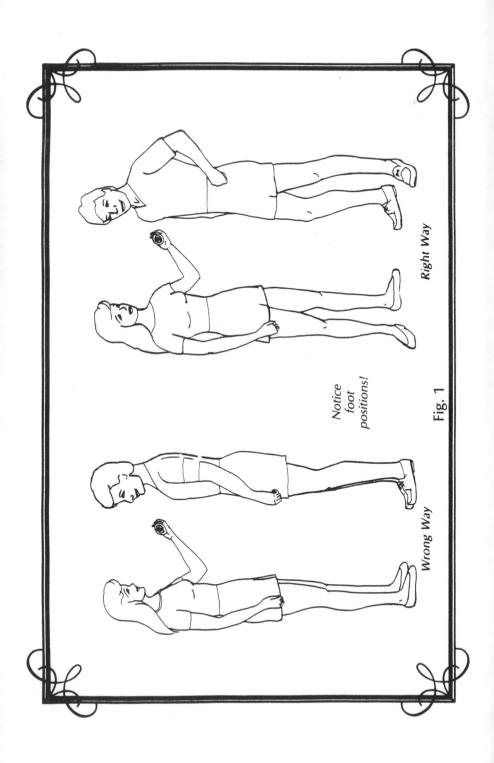

Wrong Way

Notice
foot
positions!

Right Way

Fig. 1

more slowly than usual. They should not be afraid to pause or to emphasize short phrases. However, they should not try to be "arty" or stilted. Shakespeare wrote very energetic plays.

A second main point in directing is to keep the students facing the audience, even if they are talking to someone else. They should "fake front," so that their bodies are facing the audience and their heads are only half-way towards the other actors. (Fig.1)

The cast should be told that when the announcers speak between scenes, servants can continue to change the stage set, and actors can enter, exit, or stand around pretending to talk silently. But if an announcer speaks during a scene, the actors should "freeze" until the announcer has finished his lines. At no time should the actors look at the announcers. (The announcers' parts may be cut out if the director so desires.)

Encouragement and applause inspire the young to do better, and criticism should always be linked with a compliment. Often, letting the students find their own way through the play produces the best results. And telling them, "Mean what you say," or "Be more energetic!" is all they really need.

SCHEDULES AND BUDGET

Forty-five minutes a day—using half the time for group scenes and half the time for individual scenes—is generally enough for students to rehearse. The director should encourage all to learn their lines as soon as possible. An easy way to memorize lines is to tape them and have the student listen to the tape at home each evening, going over it four or five times. Usually actors learn faster by ear than by eye. In all, it takes about six weeks to prepare a good show.

The play seems more complete if it has an audience, even other people from next door. But an afternoon or evening public performance is better yet. The director should announce the show well in advance. A PTA meeting, Open House, a Renaissance Fair, a holiday—all are excellent times to do a play.

To attract a good crowd, the admission should be very small or free. However, a Drama Fund is always useful, so some groups pass a hat, or parents sell cookies and punch. But the best way to raise money for a Drama Fund is to sell advertising in the program. A business-card size ad can sell for $5 to $10, and a larger ad can bring in even more. This is money gained well in advance of the show. It can be used for costumes or small 250-500 cwatt spotlights that can be mounted anywhere. Until there is money in the Drama Fund, the director often becomes an expert at borrowing and improvising. Fortunately, Shakespeare's plays can be produced with almost no scenery or special costumes, and there are no royalties to pay.

SPECIAL NOTES ON THIS PLAY

Macbeth is designed to have relatively simple staging: two "wings" or screens on each side of the stage area, and a curtained alcove across the back. If the school has a stage, fine. But good shows can take place at one end of a room.

What can people use as screens? Tall cardboard refrigerator boxes are good. Stage flats, frames of 1" x 4" lumber joined by triangles of plywood and covered with muslin sheeting, are excellent if little side flats are hinged to the

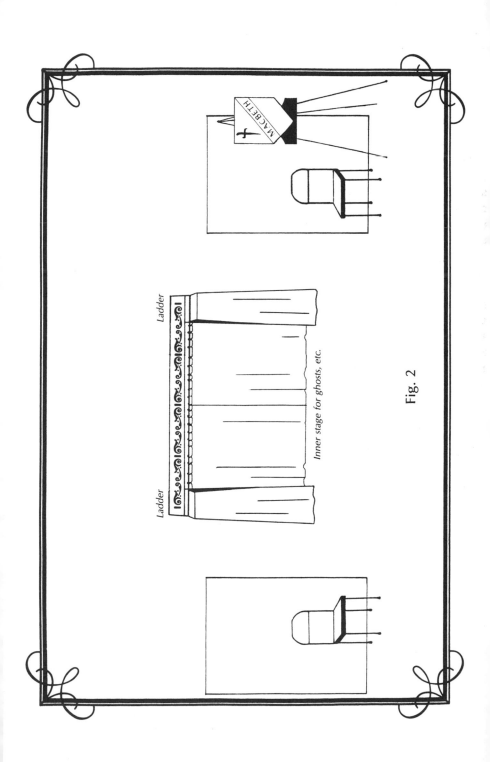

Ladder

Ladder

Inner stage for ghosts, etc.

MACBETH

Fig. 2

main one, to provide bracing. The curtain along the back is necessary for the King's murder, the ghost, and the witches' cauldron scene. Two six- or eight-foot ladders can make the basis for the alcove. A pole between the ladders will support curtains made of two sheets, especially if the ladders are weighted with buckets of bricks to keep them from tipping over. Two additional sheets hide the ladders, and a decorative cardboard header gives a finished look. Aluminum duct tape holds sheets and cardboard best. A bench, table, stools, and a throne can be added as needed. (Fig. 2)

There are two basic sets for the play: wild outdoor scenes and castle interiors. Bare branches or bushes can indicate outdoor sets, and various banners can show the different castles: one each for Duncan, Macbeth, Macduff, and one for England. (Fig. 3) A servant can hang a banner on a screen or easel, changing it when necessary.

The director should decide where actors enter and exit, having one side of the stage lead to the battleground and England, and the other side to Macbeth's castle, so that people come and go logically.

On each side of the stage should be chairs where the two announcers sit during the scenes.

Macbeth takes simple Dark Ages costumes, which are almost the same as Roman or Bibical costumes: a long-sleeved tunic for the men, belted at the waist, with either a medium or long skirt. The women wear the same with a long skirt. The men also wear broadswords. Cloaks are gathered on one shoulder with an elaborate pin. The women wear a jeweled headband or veil. The Witches have beards but no pointed hats; false noses, black teeth and freak wigs are appropriate, however.

The show of Eight Kings can be done with painted heads on sticks. Banquo can mount a ladder to point to them.

BANNERS

Duncan's Castle

Macbeth's Castle

Macduff's Castle

England

Fig. 3

Macbeth's severed head at the end can be a styrofoam wig "head" painted to look like Macbeth.

A word of warning is necessary: all sword-fights should be carefully rehearsed, with much waving of swords at a distance and little actual combat. Students should be very careful not to play with even imitation swords or daggers, as someone may be hurt.

Background music might include Moussourghsky's *Night on Bald Mountain* or Grieg's *Hall of the Mountain King.*

A LAST BIT OF ADVICE

How will the director know if he has produced Shakespeare "correctly"? He can ask his group if they had fun. If they answer, "Yes," then the show is a success!

CHARACTERS

Two Announcers (optional), who have been added

The Royal Family
    Duncan, the old King of Scotland
    Prince Malcolm, Duncan's older son
    Prince Donalbain (**Don**-ul-bane), Duncan's
        younger son

Nobles and Ladies
    Macbeth, Thane of Glamis, an ambitious hero
    Lady Macbeth, Macbeth's evil wife
    Banquo (**Ban**-kwo), Macbeth's friend
    Fleance (**Flay**-ahnce), Banquo's young son
    Macduff, a noble loyal to Prince Malcolm
    Lady Macduff, Macduff's dear wife
    Young Macduff, a little child
    Lennox, a young noble
    Ross, a noble
    Angus, Menteith, Caithness and Siward, warriors
    A Gentlewoman, Lady Macbeth's lady-in-waiting

Attendants
    Bleeding Sergeant
    Drunken Porter
    Three Hired Murderers
    Doctor
    Seyton, Macbeth's guard
    Lords, Ladies, Servants, Soldiers, etc.

Ghosts and Spirits
    Three Witches
    Three Apparitions or Spirits

ACT I

(A leafless tree indicates an outdoor scene. The two announcers enter, bow, and take their places on each side of the stage area.)

Announcer 1: (To the audience) Welcome, everyone, to a production of Shakespeare's *Macbeth*, given by the _____ class.

Announcer 2: This is not the complete play but a very short edition for young people, using the original words.

Announcer 1: We two announcers have been added to the play to help explain any hard parts.

Announcer 2: You will notice some long words, because in Shakespeare's time, people liked to play with big words as a sort of game with sounds.

Announcer 1: The story takes place in Scotland in the Dark Ages, when the world is filled with sword-fights, witches, ghosts, wars and murder.

Announcer 2: At this time Scotland is fighting two wars at one time: a rebellion and a Viking invasion. But it has a great general named Macbeth defending it. *(He points offstage.)*

Announcer 1: However, three witches meet near the battlefield with plans for the hero Macbeth.

(The two announcers sit as the three witches fly in on broomsticks. Thunder sounds.)

First Witch: When shall we three meet again? In thunder, lightning, or in rain?

Second Witch: (Pointing to the offstage battle.) When the hurly-burly's done, when the battle's lost and won.

Third Witch: (Squinting at the dark sky.) That will be ere the set of sun.

First Witch: Where the place?

Second Witch: (Pointing again.) Upon the heath.

Third Witch: There to meet with . . . Macbeth!

Announcer 2: The witches describe the world as a place full of false appearances, where good things look bad and bad things look good.

All Witches: (Joining hands and dancing around.) Fair is foul and foul is fair! Hover through the fog and filthy air!

(They fly off together, as a trumpet announces Old King Duncan, his son Prince Malcolm and young Prince Donalbain. With them are Lennox and some soldiers. From the battleground comes crawling a bleeding Sergeant.)

Announcer 1: Duncan, the old King of Scotland, wants to hear how the war against the rebels is going.

Duncan: What bloody man is that? He can report of the revolt the newest state.

Malcolm: (Kneeling by the Sergeant) Hail, brave friend! Say to the King thy knowledge of the broil as thou didst leave it.

Sergeant: (Pointing off towards the battle.) Doubtful it stood. The merciless Macdonwald from the Western Isles is supplied. But all's too weak. For brave Macbeth—well he deserves that name!—carved out his passage till he faced the slave. *(The Sergeant points to his own body to show how Macbeth cut the rebel chief from his navel to jaws and then took off his head.)* He "un-seamed" him from the nave to the chops and fixed his head upon our battlements! *(Everyone cheers.)*

Announcer 2: This leaves only the Viking invasion from Norway for Macbeth to fight.

Sergeant: (Waving a weak hand) Mark, King of Scotland, mark! No sooner justice had compelled these kerns to trust their heels, but the **Norweyan** lord began a fresh assault! *(The Sergeant collapses.)* But I am faint. My gashes cry for help!

Duncan: Go. Get him surgeons! *(As soldiers carry off the Sergeant, two nobles with bloody swords, Ross and Angus, arrive.)* Who comes here?

Malcolm: The worthy Thane of Ross. *(He rushes to lead Ross to his father. Ross kneels briefly.)*

Duncan: Whence camest thou, worthy thane?

Ross: (Pointing to the battlefield) From Fife, great King, where the Norweyan banners fan our people cold. Norway himself, with terrible numbers, assisted by the Thane of Cawdor, began a dismal conflict!

Announcer 1: We now hear how Macbeth also defeated the King from Norway and the traitor Cawdor.

Ross: (Continuing) Till that "Bellona's bridegroom" confronted him . . . *(He waves his sword as if fighting.)* . . . point against point, and to conclude . . . the victory fell on us! *(Everyone cheers.)*

Announcer 2: The King plans to give Macbeth a reward—the title and riches of the rebel Thane of Cawdor.

Duncan: No more that Thane of Cawdor shall deceive our bosom interest. Go, pronounce his present death, and with his former title greet Macbeth! *(All cheer.)*

Ross: I'll see it done! *(He kneels and then leaves quickly with Angus to return to the battlefield.)*

Duncan: What he hath lost, noble Macbeth hath won!

(The King and court leave in the opposite direction.)

Announcer 1: But then the Witches meet Macbeth . . .

(A howling wind and loud shrieks accompany the Three Witches, who fly in on their brooms.)

First Witch: (To Second Witch) Where has thou been, sister?

Second Witch: (Picking her teeth) Killing swine. *(A drum begins to beat slowly.)*

Third Witch: A drum, a drum! Macbeth doth come!

All Witches: (Joining hands, they circle back and forth.) The weird sisters, hand in hand, posters of the sea and land, thus do go about, about. Thrice to thine, and thrice to mine, and thrice again, to make up nine. *(They stop suddenly.)* Peace! The charm's wound up!

(They hide as Macbeth and his friend Banquo enter. Macbeth carries a Viking helmet like a war trophy.)

Macbeth: (Gazing around at the dark day.) So foul and fair a day I have not seen! *(He puts up his sword and looks at the helmet happily. The Witches creep up and startle the men with wild laughter.)*

Banquo: What are these, so withered and so wild in their attire? *(He looks at them with curiosity.)* Live you? *(The Witches say, "Sssh!")* You seem to understand me, by each at once her chappy finger laying upon her skinny lips. You should be women, and yet your beards forbid me to interpret that you are so.

Macbeth: Speak, if you can. What are you? *(He draws back when the Witches spring at him, one by one, as they tell his fortune.)*

First Witch: All hail, Macbeth! Hail to thee, Thane of Glamis!

Second Witch: All hail, Macbeth! Hail to thee, Thane of Cawdor!

Third Witch: All hail, Macbeth, that shalt be **King** hereafter! *(Macbeth backs off, frightened.)*

Banquo: Good sir, why do you start and seem to fear things that do sound so fair? *(To the Witches, holding out his hand to have his fortune told too.)* To me you speak not. If you can look into the Seeds of Time, speak then to me!

First Witch: (Dancing around Banquo) Hail!

Second Witch: Hail!

Third Witch: Hail!

First Witch: (Teasing him with a riddle.) Lesser **than** Macbeth and greater!

Second Witch: Not so happy, yet much happier!

Third Witch: Thou shalt **get** Kings, though **thou be** none! So all hail, Macbeth and Banquo!

First Witch: Banquo and Macbeth, all hail!

Announcer 2: So Macbeth will be King, **and Banquo** will "beget" or be a father to many **kings.**

Macbeth: I know I am Thane of Glamis. But how of Cawdor? The Thane of Cawdor lives. And to be King stands not within the prospect of belief. Speak, I charge you! *(The Witches clap their hands, momentarily blinding the men, and rush off.)*

Banquo: (Rubbing his eyes) Whither are they vanished?

Macbeth: Into the air. *(He looks about.)*

Banquo: (Laughing uneasily) Were such things here as we do speak about?

Macbeth: (Seriously) Your children shall be Kings!

Banquo: (Joking) You shall be King!

Macbeth: And Thane of Cawdor too. Went it not so?

Banquo: To the selfsame tune and words. *(He looks off and sees Ross and Angus enter.)* Who's here?

Ross: (Shaking hands with Macbeth) The King hath happily received, Macbeth, the news of thy success! And he bade me call thee . . . Thane of Cawdor!

Macbeth: (Suspiciously) The Thane of Cawdor lives.

Angus: Treasons have overthrown him!

Macbeth: (To himself, almost day-dreaming.) Glamis, and Thane of Cawdor! *(He looks at the Viking helmet as if it is a crown.)* The greatest is behind. *(To Ross and Angus, pleasantly.)* Thanks for your pains! *(To Banquo, whispering)* Do you not hope your children shall be Kings? *(Banquo shrugs.)*

Banquo: *(Taking out a map)* Cousins, a word, I pray you! *(He, Ross and Angus look at the map, while Macbeth walks to one side, thinking to himself.)*

Announcer 1: Macbeth is shaken by the new title that the witches predicted. He thinks of being King, and he thinks of murder too.

Macbeth: This supernatural soliciting cannot be ill, cannot be good. I am Thane of Cawdor! *(He holds out his hand and watches it shake.)* My thought, whose murder yet is but fantastical, shakes my state of man. And nothing is but what is not!

Banquo: *(Looking up from the map.)* Look, how our partner's rapt! *(Ross and Angus laugh.)*

Macbeth: *(Rousing himself)* Kind gentlemen, let us' toward the King. Come, friends! *(They exit.)*

Announcer 2: At this time, any noblemen might be the next king if Old King Duncan gives him a special title: the Prince of Cumberland. No one knows who will be chosen the next Prince of Cumberland.

(Meanwhile, servants take off the tree and bring on Duncan's banner. Duncan, Lennox, Malcolm, and Donalbain enter.)

Duncan: *(Looking off, he sees Macbeth, Banquo, Ross and Angus enter. He greets Macbeth eagerly.)* O worthiest cousin! Welcome hither. *(He embraces*

Banquo.) Noble Banquo, let me hold thee to my heart! *(Macbeth gives the King the helmet.)*

(The King then stands in the center, alone. A trumpet sounds. The courtiers become quiet, and Macbeth looks tense. The King holds up the Viking helmet and makes an announcement.) Sons, kinsmen, thanes, and you whose places are the nearest! Know, we will establish our estate . . . *(He smiles at his oldest son.)* . . . upon our eldest, **Malcolm**, whom we name . . . the Prince of Cumberland! *(Malcolm kneels before his father. The King puts the Viking helmet like a crown on his son's head. Macbeth looks furious. The courtiers applaud.)*

Announcer 1: So Macbeth will not be the next king as he had hoped. Young Malcolm has been chosen. But King Duncan will honor Macbeth with a visit to his castle.

Duncan: (To Macbeth) From hence to Inverness, and bind us further to you!

Macbeth: (Trying to be polite) I'll make joyful the hearing of my wife with your approach. *(He kneels and turns to go.)*

Duncan: (With affection.) My worthy Cawdor!

Macbeth: (Glaring back at Malcolm, who is admiring the Viking helmet.) The Prince of Cumberland! *(To the sky, secretly)* Stars, hide your fires. Let not light see my black and deep desires! *(He leaves hurriedly, followed by the King and court.)*

Announcer 2: While Macbeth is riding home, Lady Macbeth reads a letter that he has sent her.

(Servants carry on Macbeth's banner. Lady Macbeth enters, reading a scroll.)

Lady Macbeth: "They met me in the day of success. When I burned to question them further, they made themselves air. Whiles I stood rapt in wonder, came missives from the King, who hailed me 'Thane of Cawdor,' by which title, before, these weird sisters saluted me and referred me to the coming-on of time with 'Hail, **King** that shalt be!' My dearest partner of greatness, lay it to thy heart and farewell!"

(She presses the letter to her heart and speaks in a strong voice.) Glamis thou art, and Cawdor,and **shalt be** what thou art promised! *(But she looks doubtful, because Macbeth has a soft streak.)* Yet I do fear thy nature. It is too full o' the "milk of human kindness" to catch the nearest way. *(She turns quickly as an excited attendant enters.)* What is your tidings?

Attendant: The King comes here tonight!

Lady Macbeth: (Alert) Is not thy master with him?

Attendant: (Waving a hand behind him as hoofbeats sound.) So please you, our thane is **coming!**

Lady Macbeth: He brings great news! *(The attendant runs off.)*

Announcer 1: Lady Macbeth calls on the spirits of evil to help her commit murder.

Lady Macbeth: (Looking upward) Come, you spirits, and fill me from the crown to the toe, top-full of direst cruelty! *(She draws a dagger.)* Come, thick night, that my keen knife see not the wound it makes. Nor Heaven peep through the blanket of the dark to cry, "Hold, hold!" *(Macbeth enters, and she runs to him eagerly.)* Great Glamis! Worthy Cawdor!

Macbeth: (Hugging her) My dearest love, Duncan comes here tonight!

Lady Macbeth: (With a smile, she shows her dagger.) And when goes hence?

Macbeth: (Uneasily) Tomorrow.

Lady Macbeth: (Stabbing at the air as if it is Duncan.) O, never shall sun that morrow see!

(Macbeth frowns, and she smooths out his wrinkles gently.) Your face, my thane, is as a book where men may read strange matters. Look like the innocent flower, but **be** the serpent under it! *(She pats her dagger.)* And you shall put this night's great business into **my** dispatch! *(She hugs him with joy but Macbeth looks away, as if uncertain.)*

Macbeth: We will speak further!

Lady Macbeth: Leave all the rest to me!

(They leave together as trumpets sound. The King enters with Banquo, Ross, Lennox and others. The King looks around at the scenery.)

Announcer 2: The King arrives at the Macbeth's castle.

Duncan: This castle hath a pleasant seat!

Banquo: The air is delicate.

Duncan: (As Lady Macbeth enters and curtsies.) See, see, our honored hostess! *(She looks at him and seems startled suddenly, but then she smiles.)* Fair and noble hostess, we are your guest tonight!

Lady Macbeth: Your servants ever! *(They go into the castle together, smiling and friendly.)*

Announcer 1: A feast follows, celebrating the end of the wars. But Macbeth is still thinking about murder. Should he or should he not kill the King?

(Several servants carry food and drink across the stage. Macbeth enters from the banquet, and he draws out his dagger, thinking aloud.)

Macbeth: If it were done when 'tis done, then 'twere well it were done quickly. *(He shakes his head.)* He's here in double trust. First, as I am his kinsman. Then as his host, who should against his murderer shut the door, not bear the knife myself. Besides, this Duncan hath borne his faculties so meek, that tears shall drown the wind! I have no spur but only vaulting ambition!

Lady Macbeth: (Entering angrily.) Why have you left the chamber?

Macbeth: (Firmly putting his dagger away.) We will proceed no further in this business. He hath honored me of late.

Lady Macbeth: (Sneering) Art thou afeard? Wouldst thou live a coward?

Macbeth: (Shouting) Prithee, peace!

Lady Macbeth: (Shouting back) When you durst do it, **then** you were a man!

Macbeth: (Hesitating) If we should fail . . . ?

Lady Macbeth: We fail? *(She gives a harsh laugh.)* But screw your courage to the sticking-place, and we'll not fail!

Announcer 2: Lady Macbeth plans to drug the King's guards and blame them for the King's murder.

Lady Macbeth: When Duncan is asleep, what cannot you and I perform? What not put upon his officers?

Macbeth: Will it not be received, when we have marked with blood those sleepy two of his own chamber and used their daggers, that **they** have done it?

Lady Macbeth: (Smiling happily) Who dares receive it other?

Macbeth: *(With determination)* I am settled! *(He takes her arm to return to the feast.)* Away! False face must hide what the false heart doth know! *(Sounds of wind and thunder rise and die down.)*

ACT II

Announcer 1: Late at night, after the feast is over, the King and nobles go to bed.

(Lady Macbeth ushers the sleepy King and two servants to a bedroom behind the center curtains. Banquo and his young son, Fleance, also enter.)

Banquo: How goes the night, boy? *(They look up.)*

Fleance: The moon is down. I have not heard the clock.

Banquo: Hold, take my sword. *(He hands his sword to the lad, but a noise makes him snatch it back.)* Give me my sword! *(Calling)* Who's there?

Macbeth: (Entering with a servant) A friend.

Banquo: What, sir, not yet at rest? The King's a-bed. *(With an awkward pause.)* I dreamt last night of the three weird sisters.

Macbeth: (Shrugging) I think not of them. Good repose the while!

Banquo: The like to you. *(He and Fleance leave.)*

Announcer 2: It is almost time for the murder, and Macbeth starts seeing things that are not there.

Macbeth: Is this a dagger which I see before me,
the handle toward my hand?

Macbeth: (To the servant) Go bid thy mistress, when my drink is ready, she strike upon the bell. *(The servant bows and leaves. A drum beats softly. Macbeth looks up amazed at something in the air.)*

Is this a dagger which I see before me, the handle toward my hand? *(He reaches for it.)* Come, let me clutch thee! *(His hand closes on nothing.)* I have thee not, and yet I see thee still! *(He covers his face with his hands and then looks out again, frightened.)* I see thee still. And on thy blade and dudgeon . . . gouts of blood, which was not so before! *(He shouts.)* There's no such thing!

(Looking around at the dark.) Now, o'er the one-half world, Nature seems dead. And wicked dreams abuse the curtained sleep. Now Witchcraft celebrates. And withered Murder moves like a ghost. *(The drum beats faster.)*

(A bell rings, Lady Macbeth's signal that all is clear. Macbeth draws his dagger and leaves slowly.) I go, and it is done. The bell invites me. *(Calling softly)* Hear it not, Duncan! For it is a knell that summons thee to Heaven or to Hell!

(He opens the center curtains. Lady Macbeth appears and motions him inside. She closes the curtains and rubs her hands nervously. A bird cries and she is startled.)

Lady Macbeth: Hark! Peace! *(Relaxing)* It was the owl that shrieked. *(Looking back)* He is about it!

Macbeth: (From inside) Who's there? What, ho!

Lady Macbeth: Alack, I am afraid they have awaked and 'tis not done! I laid their daggers ready. He could not miss 'em. *(Rubbing her hands, she starts to sob with fright.)* Had he not resembled **my father** as he slept, I had done it! *(The drum stops suddenly. Macbeth enters, horrified. In his hand he holds two bloody daggers.)* My husband!

Macbeth: I have done the deed! Didst thou not hear a noise?

Lady Macbeth: I heard the owl scream and the crickets cry.

Macbeth: (Shaking his head, he looks at the bloody daggers.) This is a sorry sight!

Lady Macbeth: Consider it not so deeply! So, it will make us mad!

Macbeth: (As if hysterical) Methought I heard a voice cry, "Sleep no more! Macbeth does murder sleep!" The innocent sleep. Sleep that knits up the ravelled sleave of care. *(He shudders.)*

Lady Macbeth: (Alarmed) What do you mean?

Macbeth: Still it cried, "Sleep no more!" to all the house. "Macbeth shall sleep no more!" *(He puts his arm across his face.)*

Lady Macbeth: Go get some water and wash. *(She sees the daggers.)* Why did you bring these daggers from the place? They must lie there! Go carry them, and smear the sleepy grooms with blood.

Macbeth: I'll go no more. I am afraid to think what I have done. Look on it again I dare not.

Lady Macbeth: (With scorn) Give me the daggers! *(Taking the weapons, she goes into the bedchamber. From the castle gate comes sudden knocking.)*

Macbeth: Whence is that knocking? *(He raises his bloody hands and stares at them as if they belong to someone else.)* What hands are here? *(As his hands come closer.)* Ha! They pluck out mine eyes!

Lady Macbeth: (Returning from the death room with bloody hands, she looks weak and frightened.) My hands are of your color, but I shame to wear a heart so white. *(They cling to each other. More knocking rouses them.)* I hear a knocking at the south entry. Retire we to our chamber. A little water clears us of this deed. How easy is it then!

Macbeth: (Calling out to the gate.) Wake Duncan with thy knocking! I would thou couldst! *(They exit.)*

Announcer 1: But King Duncan is dead. He cannot be waked. However, the knocking does wake somebody—a very drunk porter.

Porter: (Staggering on) Here's a knocking indeed! *(He takes a drink from a jug as the knocking continues. He shouts back at it.)* Knock, knock, knock! Who's there, in the name of Beelzebub? *(Knocking again)* Knock, knock! Who's there, in the other devil's name? *(He hiccups.)* But this place is too cold for Hell. *(He goes to the side and pretends to open a door, putting out his hand for a tip.)* I pray you, remember the porter! *(Two nobles, Macduff and Lennox, enter.)*

Macduff: Is thy master stirring? *(Macbeth returns, his face and hands washed.)* Our knocking has awaked him. Is the King stirring, worthy thane?

Macbeth: Not yet. I'll bring you to him. *(He leads Macduff to the curtains and holds them open for him to enter. Macbeth and Lennox stay outside.)*

Lennox: (Politely talking about the storm.) The night has been unruly. Where we lay, our chimneys were blown down. Some say the earth did shake!

Macbeth: (Grimly) 'Twas a rough night!

Macduff: (Appearing, almost speechless with shock.) O horror, horror, horror!

Lennox: What's the matter?

Macduff: (Pointing inside the curtains.) Most sacrilegious murder . . .

Lennox: Mean you his Majesty?

Macduff: (Motioning them inside) See, and then speak yourselves! *(Macbeth and Lennox rush inside as Banquo calls out loudly.)* Awake, awake! Ring the alarum-bell! Murder and treason! Banquo and Donalbain! Malcolm! *(A bell begins to ring loudly.)* Awake and look on death itself!

(Lady Macbeth appears in a dressing gown as if just awakened. Banquo rushes on also.) O Banquo, Banquo, our royal master's murdered!

Lady Macbeth: (Over-acting) What, in **our** house?

Banquo: (Rudely) Too cruel anywhere.

> *(Macbeth returns with Lennox from the death chamber while the princes, Malcolm and Donalbain, rush in with swords drawn.)*

Donalbain: What is amiss?

Macduff: Your royal father's murdered!

Malcolm: (Waving his sword) O, by whom?

Lennox: Those of his chamber, it seemed, had done it. Their hands and faces were all badged with blood. So were their daggers.

Macbeth: O, I do repent me that I did kill them! *(He parts the curtains. The dead King is lying on a cot with the two servants dead on the floor.)*

Lady Macbeth: Help me hence, ho! *(She faints.)*

Banquo: (To some guards) Look to the lady! *(Two men carry her out. Banquo draws the curtain in front of the dead. He turns to the others.)* Let us meet and question this most bloody piece of work!

All: Well contented! *(They exit. Prince Malcolm and his brother Donalbain are left alone.)*

Malcolm: (To Donalbain, frightened) What will you do? Let's not consort with them. I'll to England!

Donalbain: To Ireland, I!

Malcolm: Therefore to horse. And let us shift away!
(After they leave, a cheer comes from offstage.)

Announcer 2: So the Princes run away, frightened.
And the hero Macbeth is elected King of Scotland
by the noblemen, although Prince Malcolm was
supposed to have the crown.

ACT III

Announcer 1: To celebrate Macbeth's election as king, he has a feast.

(Macbeth and Lady Macbeth enter, wearing crowns. Macbeth now uses the royal word "we" when he speaks of himself. Many lords and ladies follow them. The Macbeths do not look happy, but Macbeth smiles at Banquo, who does not smile back.)

Macbeth: Here's our chief guest! Tonight we hold a solemn supper, sir. And I'll request your presence.

Banquo: (With a formal bow) Let your Highness command upon me. *(Macbeth's smile freezes a little.)*

Announcer 2: Banquo is a problem, for his children will be kings, according to the witches.

Announcer 1: So Macbeth plans another murder.

Macbeth: Ride you this afternoon?

Banquo: Ay, my good lord.

Macbeth: Fail not our feast!

Banquo: My lord, I will not.

Macbeth: Goes Fleance with you?

Banquo: Ay, my good lord.

Macbeth: I wish your horses swift and sure of foot. Farewell. *(To all, dismissing them till dinnertime.)* Let every man be master of his time till seven at night. *(Lady Macbeth starts to speak to him, but he cuts her off too.)* We will keep ourself till suppertime alone. *(Everyone also leaves except one attendant, to whom Macbeth speaks in a low, secret voice.)* Attend those men our pleasure?

Attendant: They are, my lord, without the palace gate. *(He points off to one side.)*

Macbeth: Bring them before us. *(The attendant bows and leaves. Macbeth walks up and down, thinking aloud.)* Our fears in Banquo stick deep. They hailed him father to a line of Kings, no son of mine succeeding! *(He hears footsteps.)* Who's there? *(The two murderers enter.)* Both of you know Banquo was your enemy?

Both Murderers: True, my lord.

Macbeth: So is he mine. It must be done tonight. *(He gives money to the men.)* And with him . . . Fleance, his son, that keeps him company. *(He makes a gesture of cutting his throat. The murderers nod with understanding.)*

Both Murderers: We are resolved, my lord. *(They bow and leave.)*

Macbeth: (With relief) It is concluded. *(Calling out to the sky.)* Banquo, thy soul's flight, if it find Heaven, must find it out tonight. *(He follows the murderers off.)*

(Lady Macbeth enters from the other side, looking about as if for Macbeth. A servant enters.)

Lady Macbeth: Say to the King, I would attend his leisure for a few words.

Servant: (Bowing) Madam, I will. *(He leaves.)*

Announcer 2: Now the Macbeths are King and Queen, they find they are unhappy. And they are not close partners as they used to be.

Announcer 1: Macbeth even envies dead King Duncan, who has no more troubles.

Lady Macbeth: (To Macbeth, who enters and sits on the bench, not looking at her.) How now, my lord? Why do you keep alone? *(Nervously)* What's done is done!

Macbeth: (Taking off his crown and rubbing his head as if it aches.) Duncan is in his grave. After life's fitful fever, **he** sleeps well. Treason has done his worst. Nor steel, nor poison, malice domestic, foreign levy—nothing can touch him further.

Lady Macbeth: (Trying to cheer him up) Gentle my lord, be bright among your guests tonight!

Macbeth: So shall I, love. And so, I pray, be you. *(But he breaks down and holds his head.)* O, full of scorpions is my mind, dear wife! *(He looks miserable.)* Thou knowst that Banquo and his Fleance live . . .

Lady Macbeth: (Suspicious) What's to be done?

Macbeth: (Patting her cheek) Be innocent of the knowledge, dearest chuck. *(He rises and takes her by the hand.)* So, prithee, go with me . . . *(They leave, both looking haunted.)*

Announcer 2: As night falls, the murderers gather to ambush Banquo and his son Fleance.

(A servant removes the banner. Other servants bring on two bushes. As they leave, the three murderers enter and hide behind the bushes.)

First Murderer: (To Third Murderer) But who did bid thee join with us?

Third Murderer: Macbeth. *(There is the sound of hoofbeats.)* Hark! I hear horses!

Banquo: (Calling from offstage) Give us a light there, ho! *(He enters with Fleance, who carries a torch.)*

Third Murderer: (Whispering) 'Tis he!

Banquo: (Looking at the sky) It will be rain tonight.

First Murderer: (With a shout) Let it come down!

(The murderers set upon Banquo, slashing at his head. They knock the torch from Fleance's hand. Banquo shouts for his son to run away.)

Banquo: Fly, good Fleance, fly, fly, fly! *(Fleance runs off as Banquo dies.)*

Third Murderer: There's but one down. The son is fled!

First Murderer: (Shrugging) Well, let's away and say how much is done. *(They go off, dragging Banquo.)*

(Servants remove the bushes and bring on Macbeth's banner, a throne, a long table, and stools to put behind the table. Meanwhile the Macbeths, with their lords and ladies, enter and stand talking, as if at a banquet.)

Announcer 1: The great celebration is ready to start.

Announcer 2: And Banquo was ordered to come.

Macbeth: (To everyone) Sit down! At first and last, the hearty welcome!

Lords: Thanks to your Majesty. *(They sit, leaving an empty stool in the center, before the curtain.)*

Macbeth: (Speaking of himself) Ourself will mingle with society, and play the humble host. *(He leads his wife to the throne.)* Our hostess keeps her state.

Lady Macbeth: My heart speaks they are welcome!

(The First Murderer appears at the edge of the stage and waves a little to Macbeth, who nods.)

Macbeth: (Pointing to the empty stool.) Here I'll sit in the midst. *(He motions to a servant, who brings wine cups.)* Anon we'll drink a measure the table round. *(As the servant passes the wine, Macbeth slowly drifts to the Murderer and speaks in a harsh whisper.)* There's blood upon thy face.

First Murderer: 'Tis Banquo's then. My lord, his throat is cut.

Macbeth: Thou art the best of the cutthroats! Yet he's good that did the like for Fleance.

First Murderer: (Ashamed) Most royal sir, Fleance is escaped.

Macbeth: (Angrily) But Banquo's safe?

First Murderer: Ay, my good lord. Safe in a ditch. With twenty trenched gashes on his head.

Macbeth: Thanks for that. *(He gives the man a bag of money.)* Get thee gone. *(The murderer nods and leaves, as Macbeth returns to the table, where he raises a goblet of wine in a toast.)* Now, good digestion wait on appetite, and health to both! *(All clink glasses and drink.)*

(The Ghost of Banquo glides from between the curtains and sits on Macbeth's stool in the middle. His head is covered with the twenty gashes. No one can see him except Macbeth.)

Lennox: (Waving to the stool) May it please your Highness sit?

Macbeth: (To the Ghost) Thou canst not say I did it!
Never shake thy gory locks at me!

Macbeth: (Looking around casually) The table's full.

Lennox: (Pointing to the Ghost) Here is a place reserved, sir!

Macbeth: (Puzzled) Where?

Lennox: Here, my good lord. *(Macbeth sees the Ghost and drops his wine cup in fear.)* What is it that moves your Highness?

Macbeth: (Thinking the Ghost is a trick.) Which of you have done this? *(The Ghost shakes his head.)*

Lords: (In amazement) What, my good lord?

Macbeth: (To the Ghost) Thou canst not say I did it! Never shake thy gory locks at me!

Ross: (Standing, astonished) Gentlemen, rise. His Highness is not well!

Lady Macbeth: (Trying to quiet them) Sit, worthy friends. *(She takes Macbeth to one side and scolds him.)* Are you a man?

Macbeth: (Pointing to the Ghost with a shaking hand.) Ay, and a bold one, that dare look on that which might appal the devil!

Lady Macbeth: O proper stuff! This is the very painting of your fear. Why do you make such faces? When all's done, you look but on a stool.

Macbeth: (Pointing at the Ghost) See there! Behold! Look! Lo! *(The Ghost vanishes, and Macbeth swears an oath.)* If I stand here, I **saw** him!

Lady Macbeth: For shame! *(Pulling him to the table.)* My worthy lord, your noble friends do lack you.

Macbeth: (Taking a new glass of wine.) I drink to the general joy of the whole table and . . . *(Nervously smiling)* . . . to our dear friend Banquo, whom we miss. Would he were here! *(The Ghost comes back at this invitation. Macbeth bellows at him in fear.)* Avaunt! And quit my sight! Let the earth hide thee! Hence, horrible shadow! *(The Ghost disappears, but the guests all rise and whisper.)*

Lady Macbeth: (Motioning for the guests to depart.) He grows worse and worse. At once, good night. Go at once! *(The guests leave, looking suspicious.)*

Macbeth: (He sinks into the throne and looks at the floor, his eyes hollow.) It will have blood! They say, blood will have blood! *(He arrives at a decision.)* I will tomorrow to the weird sisters. More shall they speak!

Lady Macbeth: (Rubbing her hands) You lack the season of all natures, sleep.

Macbeth: Come, we'll to sleep. *(He looks again at the place where the Ghost was, and he shudders.)*

(They leave sadly. Servants remove the furniture. The three witches enter with a big cooking pot, their witch's cauldron, which they put before the center curtain.)

ACT IV

Announcer 1: The next day, Macbeth goes to the witches' cave.

Announcer 2: There the witches brew powerful magic in their cauldron or cooking pot. The ingredients include poisoned guts, a toad, and poisoned sweat.

First Witch: (As they dance and sing or recite.)
Round about the cauldron go.
In the poisoned entrails throw.
Toad, that under cold stone
Days and nights has thirty-one.
Sweltered venom sleeping got,
Boil thou first in the charmed pot!

All: (Dancing around wildly)
Double, double, toil and trouble.
Fire, burn! And cauldron, bubble!

Announcer 1: Next come parts of a snake, newt, frog, bat, dog, a snake's tongue, a sting of a legless lizard, a lizard's leg and a baby owl's wing.

Second Witch: Fillet of a fenny snake
In the cauldron boil and bake!
Eye of newt and toe of frog,
Wool of bat and tongue of dog.

WITCHES' SONG

Adder's fork and blind-worm's sting,
Lizard's leg and howlet's wing,
For a charm of powerful trouble,
Like a hell-broth, boil and bubble!

All: Double, double, toil and trouble.
Fire, burn! And cauldron, bubble!

Third Witch: (Throwing in the last bit.)
Cool it with a baboon's blood.
Then the charm is firm and good!

Second Witch: (Looking at her knobby hands.) By the
pricking of my thumbs, something wicked this
way comes! *(She throws her arms up as she
shouts.)* Open, locks, whoever knocks!

*(Macbeth enters, large and dark, with a great
cloak about him. He greets the Witches harshly.)*

Macbeth: How now, you secret, black and midnight
hags! What is it you do?

All: (With a wicked cackle) A deed without a name!

Macbeth: Answer me to what I ask you!

First Witch: Say, if thou hadst rather hear it from our
mouths, or from our masters?

Macbeth: (Bravely) Call 'em. Let me see 'em!

All: (Chanting) Come, high or low—
Thyself and office deftly show!

Announcer 2: Three spirits now give Macbeth advice and fair promises.

(From between the curtains comes the first apparition or spirit, a head in a great helmet.)

First Apparition: (Chanting in a deathly voice) Macbeth, Macbeth, Macbeth! Beware Macduff! Beware the Thane of Fife! Dismiss me. Enough! *(The vision disappears.)*

Macbeth: For thy good caution, thanks!

Announcer 1: Now Macbeth must fear only Macduff.

First Witch: Here's another . . .

(Thunder roars and the second apparition appears above the cauldron, a baby with a bloody face.)

Second Apparition: (In a high, shrill voice.) Macbeth, Macbeth, Macbeth! Be bloody, bold, and resolute! For none of woman born shall harm Macbeth! *(It too disappears.)*

Announcer 2: And no man born from a woman can hurt him. Since everyone is born from a woman, Macbeth feels safe.

Macbeth: (As thunder roars again.) What is this?

(The third apparition appears—a child with a crown on his head and a small tree in his hand.)

Third Apparition: (In a loud young voice) Macbeth shall never vanquished be . . . until great Birnam

Wood to high Dunsinane Hill shall come **against** him! *(It too disappears.)*

Announcer 1: And Birnam Forest will take years to grow to Dunsinane castle, many miles away.

Announcer 2: But a question remains. Will Banquo's children still be kings?

Macbeth: Yet my heart throbs to know one thing. Tell me . . . shall Banquo's issue ever reign in this kingdom?

All: Seek to know no more!

Macbeth: (Angrily) Let me know! *(Strange music plays loudly.)* What noise is this?

(The cauldron is pulled behind the curtains. Above the curtains appear a row of King's heads with crowns, all alike, all resembling Banquo by having the same beard, etc. The eighth head has a mirror beside it.)

Macbeth: (To the First King) Thou art too like the spirit of Banquo. Down! A third is like the former. What, will the line stretch out to the crack of doom? A seventh! And yet the eighth appears, who bears a glass which shows me many more. *(Banquo also appears above the curtains and points to the heads of the Kings and to himself. Macbeth sounds desperate.)* Now I see 'tis true. For Banquo smiles upon me and points at them for his. *(To the Witches)* What, is this so?

First Witch: Ay, sir, all this is so!

(Macbeth covers his face with his hands. With a loud cry, all three Witches vanish. Offstage is heard the sound of galloping horses. Macbeth looks about and then rushes to the entrance.)

Macbeth: Come in, without there!

Lennox: (Entering fearfully) What's your grace's will?

Macbeth: I did hear the galloping of horse. Who was it came by?

Lennox: Tis two or three, my lord, that bring you word. **Macduff** is fled to England!

Macbeth: (Hot with rage) Fled to **England**!

Announcer 1: Macbeth knows Macduff has gone to help Prince Malcolm, the rightful heir to the throne.

Announcer 2: In revenge, Macbeth plans to murder Macduff's innocent family. Step by step, the former hero has become completely evil.

Macbeth: Even now, be it thought and done—the castle of Macduff I will surprise, seize upon Fife, give to the edge of the sword . . . his wife, his babes, and all unfortunate souls that trace him in his line!

(He strides offstage, leaving Lennox open-mouthed with surprise. Lennox thinks and then runs off in another direction. A servant puts up Macduff's banner. Lennox returns to meet Lady Macduff and

her little child, who have come onstage hand-in-hand. She looks at him, puzzled.)

Lennox: (Bowing to her hastily) Bless you, fair dame! I am not to you known. *(He points behind him.)* Some danger does approach you nearly! Be not found here! Hence with your little ones! *(He looks back.)* Heaven preserve you! *(He runs off.)*

Lady Macduff: (As two murderers enter with daggers.) What are these faces?

First Murderer: Where is your husband? He's a traitor!

Son: (Running to the murderer and hitting at him.) Thou liest, thou shag-eared villain!

First Murderer: What, you egg! *(He stabs the child.)*

Son: (Clutching his bloody shirt as he sinks to the ground.) He has killed me, Mother! Run away! *(The first murderer chases Lady Macduff offstage. There is a loud scream. The second murderer follows with the child's body.)*

Announcer 1: And in England, with Prince Malcolm, Macduff hears of the terrible murders.

(A servant changes the banner to one of England. Malcolm, Macduff and Ross enter. Macduff has his hands to his face with grief.)

Macduff: My children too?

Ross: Wife, children, servants—all that could be found.

Macduff: My wife killed too?

Ross: (Nodding) I have said.

Malcolm: (Sympathetically) Be comforted!

Macduff: (Looking at Malcolm) He has no children. *(To Ross again)* All my pretty ones? Did you say all? *(In helpless fury)* O hell-kite! All? What, all my pretty chickens and their dam at one fell swoop?

Malcolm: (Urging Macduff to fight for revenge.) Dispute it like a man!

Macduff: I shall do so, but I must also feel it as a man! *(Sadly shaking his head)* I cannot but remember such things were, that were most precious to me. Heaven rest them now . . .

Malcolm: Let grief convert to anger!

Macduff: (Drawing his sword as he swears revenge.) Front-to-front bring thou this fiend of Scotland and myself! Within my sword's length set him!

Malcolm: (With energy) Come, our power is ready! *(He draws his sword also.)* Macbeth is ripe for shaking! *(The three stride offstage rapidly.)*

Announcer 2: So war is declared against Macbeth. Malcolm and the English army begin the invasion of Scotland.

ACT V

Announcer 1: While Macbeth prepares for war, Lady Macbeth has been left alone in Dunsinane Castle. She walks in her sleep and acts so strangely that her lady-in-waiting has called a doctor.

(A servant brings on a bench and hangs up Macbeth's banner. The doctor and the gentlewoman enter.)

Doctor: (Doubtfully) I have two nights watched with you but can perceive no truth in your report. When was it she last walked?

Gentlewoman: Since his Majesty went into the field, I have seen her rise from her bed, throw her nightgown upon her, unlock her closet, take forth paper, fold it, write upon it, read it, afterwards seal it, and again return to bed—yet all this while in a most fast sleep.

Doctor: What, at any time, have you heard her say?

Gentlewoman: That, sir, which I will not report. *(She pulls the Doctor to one side.)* Lo, you, here she comes! And, upon my life, fast asleep!

(Lady Macbeth enters, her eyes wide open in horror, a candle in her hand.)

Lady Macbeth: (Scrubbing her hand harder) Out, damned spot! Out, I say!

Doctor: How came she by that light?

Gentlewoman: Why, it stood by her. She has light by her continually. 'Tis her command.

(Lady Macbeth puts the candle down on a bench and rubs her hands together over and over nervously.)

Doctor: Look how she rubs her hands.

Gentlewoman: It is an accustomed action with her, to seem thus washing her hands. I have known her continue in this a quarter of an hour.

Lady Macbeth: (Scrubbing at one place over and over.) Yet, here's a spot!

Doctor: Hark! She speaks! *(He takes out a notebook and pencil to write down what she says.)*

Lady Macbeth: (Scrubbing her hand harder) Out, damned spot! Out, I say! *(She listens, as if to a bell.)* One . . . two . . . why, then 'tis time to do it. *(A look of horror)* Hell is murky! *(To Macbeth, as if he were there.)* Fie, my lord, fie! A soldier and afeard? *(She shudders and scrubs.)* Yet who would have thought the old man to have had so much blood in him!

Doctor: (To the gentlewoman) Do you mark that?

Lady Macbeth: (Singing) The Thane of Fife had a wife. *(A low cry)* Where is she now? *(She scrubs more.)* What, will these hands ne'er be clean? *(She sniffs her hands.)* Here's the smell of the blood still. All the perfumes of Arabia will not sweeten this little hand! *(With deep sobs)* Oh . . . oh . . . oh!

Doctor: (Taking notes) Well, well, well . . .

Gentlewoman: Pray God it be, sir!

Lady Macbeth: (As if Macbeth is there at the murder.) Wash your hands, put on your nightgown, look not so pale! *(She becomes desperately practical.)* I tell you yet again, Banquo's buried! He cannot come out on his grave!

Doctor: Even so? *(He shakes his head.)*

Lady Macbeth: (To Macbeth, as if at Duncan's murder.) To bed, to bed! There's knocking at the gate! *(She holds out her hand to Macbeth.)* Come, come, come, come—give me your hand! *(Arguing desperately)* What's done cannot be undone! *(She hurries him off.)* To bed, to bed, to bed!

Doctor: (Closing his notebook) Unnatural deeds do breed unnatural troubles. God . . . God forgive us all! *(He gives his orders to the gentlewoman.)* Look after her, keep eyes upon her. So, good night. *(He stares at his notebook.)* I think, but dare not speak!

Gentlewoman: Good night, good Doctor!

(She leaves the Doctor, who re-reads his notes. Macbeth enters, wearing armor and speaking to a servant.)

Announcer 2: Macbeth is not afraid of Malcolm's invading army. The promises of the witches' spirits make him feel secure.

Macbeth: Bring me no more reports. *(The servant bows and exits. Macbeth talks to himself.)* Till Birnam Wood remove to Dunsinane, I cannot fear! *(With scorn)* What's the boy Malcolm? Was he not **born of woman?** The spirits have pronounced me thus: "Fear not, Macbeth. No man that's **born of woman** shall e'er have power upon thee!"

Servant: (Entering again, and pointing behind him in terror.) There is ten thousand . . .

Macbeth: Geese, villain?

Servant: (Stammering) Th-th-the English **force, so** please you.

Macbeth: (Furiously pushing the servant out the door.) Take thy face hence! *(He turns away, suddenly heartsick.)*

Announcer 1: Macbeth now realizes he will **grow old** without honor and without friends.

Macbeth: I am sick at heart . . . I have **lived long** enough. My way of life is fallen into **the sere, the** yellow leaf. And that which should **accompany** old age—as honor, love, obedience, **troops of** friends—I must not look to have. But, **in their** stead, curses—not loud but deep—mouth-**honor,** breath which the poor heart would fain **deny and** dare not. *(He sighs deeply, and then he notices the doctor.)* How does your patient, Doctor?

Doctor: Not so sick, my lord, as she is troubled with . . . *(He taps his head with meaning.)* . . . thick-coming fancies that keep her from her rest.

Announcer 2: Macbeth asks if the doctor cannot cure mental sickness caused by old sorrows. But the doctor knows Lady Macbeth has to cure herself.

Macbeth: Canst thou not minister to a mind diseased, pluck from the memory a rooted sorrow?

Doctor: Therein the patient must minister to himself.

Macbeth: (Insulting him) Throw physic to the dogs! I'll none of it! *(He takes out his sword and waves it, boasting.)* I will not be afraid of death and bane, till Birnam Forest come to Dunsinane! *(He exits, and the doctor follows.)*

Announcer 1: As Malcolm's army advances, it comes to a forest.

(Servants bring on many branches and stand them upright around the stage. Soldiers enter, led by Malcolm, Siward and Menteith.)

Siward: What wood is this before us?

Menteith: The Wood of Birnam.

Malcolm: (Giving orders to cut branches for camouflage.) Let every soldier hew him down a bough and bear it before him! *(All take branches and move off towards Dunsinane.)*

Announcer 2: So Birnam Wood begins to move towards Dunsinane. The witches' good promises to Macbeth begin to look false.

(Servants bring on Macbeth's banner. Macbeth enters with his sword out. He is followed by his guard, Seyton, who carries a candle.)

Macbeth: Hang out our banners on the outward walls! The cry is still, "They come!" *(A scream comes from the gentlewoman offstage.)* What is that noise?

Seyton: It is the cry of women, my good lord.

(He puts the candle on the bench and goes to investigate.)

Macbeth: I have almost forgot the taste of fears. *(Seyton returns sadly.)* Wherefore was that cry?

Seyton: The Queen, my lord, is dead!

Macbeth: (In a hollow voice) She should have died hereafter. There would have been a time for such a word. *(He seems to lose his will to live.)*

Announcer 1: Macbeth finally knows that he has no future. Day by day, life just leads to death.

Announcer 2: To him, life is only play-acting, noise, and violence. It has no point to it.

Macbeth: (Shaking his head slowly) Tomorrow . . . and tomorrow . . . and tomorrow creeps in this petty pace from day to day, to the last syllable of recorded time. And all our yesterdays have lighted fools the way to dusty death.

(He takes up the candle and blows it out.) Out, out, brief candle. Life's but a walking shadow, a poor player that struts and frets his hour upon the stage and then is heard no more. *(He sits hopelessly.)* It is a tale told by an idiot, full of sound and fury, signifying nothing!

Messenger: (Running in and pointing behind him in fright.) My lord, as I did stand my watch upon the hill, I looked toward Birnam, and anon, methought . . . the wood began to move!

Macbeth: (Roused to action) Liar and slave!

Messenger: Within this three mile may you see it coming! I say, a moving grove! *(He rushes off.)*

Macbeth: "Fear not, till Birnam Wood do come to Dunsinane," and now a wood **comes** toward Dunsinane!

(Seizing his sword, he roars out a desperate cry.) Ring the alarum-bell! Blow, wind! Come, wrack! At least we'll die with harness on our back!

(He starts to leave but meets a soldier and slays him easily. He gives a scornful laugh.)

Macbeth: Thou wast born of woman! But **swords** I smile at, weapons laugh to **scorn, brandished** by man that's of a woman born. *(He leaves confidently.)*

(Two groups of soldiers enter and line up to fight. Then one group throws down its swords, and the others take them captive with cheers.)

Announcer 1: Macbeth's soldiers surrender quickly. But Macduff fiercely searches the castle for Macbeth.

Macduff: *(Entering and looking after Macbeth.)* That way the noise is. *(Shouting a challenge to his wife's killer.)* Tyrant, show thy face! My wife and children's ghosts haunt me still. *(To Heaven)* Let me find him, Fortune! *(He rushes off.)*

(Malcolm and Siward and others enter, putting up their swords. They are smiling. Trumpets sound.)

Siward: This way, my lord. The castle's gently rendered. *(He reaches into a knapsack and draws forth a crown, which he hands to Malcolm, who smiles and puts it on.)* Enter, sir, the castle!

(They go across the stage but stand aside when Macbeth dashes on with Macduff at his heels.)

Macduff: *(Shouting to Macbeth)* Turn, hell-hound, turn!

Macbeth: *(Turning to face him, his sword ready.)* Get thee back! I bear a charmed life, which must not yield to "one of woman born."

Announcer 2: But the witches have tricked Macbeth again. Macduff was not "born of woman." He was taken from his dying mother in a Caesarian birth.

Macduff: *(To Macbeth)* Despair thy charm. Macduff was from his mother's womb . . . untimely ripped!

Macbeth: *(Horrified)* Accursed be that tongue that tells me so! *(He lowers his sword.)* I'll not fight with thee!

Macduff: Then yield thee, coward!

Macbeth: I will not yield, to kiss the ground before young Malcolm's feet. *(Getting ready for his last, hopeless fight.)* Lay on, Macduff! And damned be him that first cries, "Hold, enough!" *(They battle their way offstage.)*

(Ross and soldiers enter with some wounded.)

Malcolm: I would the friends we miss were safe arrived!

Siward: Some must go off. And yet, by these I see, so great a day as this is cheaply bought.

(Macduff enters, with Macbeth's head on a spear. All cheer. Macduff kneels at Malcolm's feet.)

Macduff: Hail, King! For so thou art! Behold, where stands the usurper's cursed head. The time is free! Hail, King of Scotland!

All: *(To the sound of trumpets.)* Hail, King of Scotland! *(They march off, happily cheering. The two announcers follow.)*

The End

(Editor's note: We hope you have liked this short edition of the play. Now you can enjoy the stage productions and the original full-length script even more. As you continue to study Shakespeare, you will find that he can be a pleasure all your life!)